# INDIA: DECENTRALISED PLANNING
Themes and Issues

## About the Author

**Dr. Bikash Mohan Sanyal**, at present Deputy Director (Econ. & Planning) of A.T.I. and Project Coordinator of Agro-Climatic Regional Planning (West Bengal Unit), formally belongs to West Bengal Educational Service. He has taught economics for the last 33 years at different Government Colleges as Reader in Economics. He has obtained his Ph. D. from Calcutta University in 1981 and has also won the Mahendra Nath Sarkar prize for best Ph. D. thesis of the year.

Dr. Sanyal has conducted several courses on Decentralised Planning involving different levels of functionaries of Panchayat both in West Bengal and in Tripura. He has wide knowledge of the operational aspects of Decetralised Planning of both States.

He has co-authored a book on Agro-Climatic Regional Planning titled *India: Agro Climatic Regional Planning- A New Approach to Sustainable Development*, funded by Planning Commission, Government of India.

# INDIA: DECENTRALISED PLANNING

## Themes and Issues

**B.M. SANYAL**
Deputy Director, Administrative Training Institute,
Govt. of West Bengal, Bidhannagar, Sector III,
Calcutta-91

CONCEPT PUBLISHING COMPANY PVT. LTD.
NEW DELHI-110059

**ISBN: 978-81-7022-846-2**

First Edition 2001

*Published and Printed by*

Concept
Since 1974

**Concept Publishing Company Pvt. Ltd.**
A/15-16, Commercial Block, Mohan Garden,
New Delhi-110059 (India)
*T* : 91-11-41101460
*E* : publishing@conceptpub.com, *W*: www.conceptpub.com

# PREFACE AND ACKNOWLEDGEMENTS

The title essay of this collection opens up a wide spectrum and variety of concerns which inform the contemporary topic on decentralised planning. In the process of participating in workshops, discussions and lectures on the subject I have realised some of the possible concerns inherent in the subject. All the essays in the collection have been provoked by these possibilities and therefore, display considerable variation in matter.

Since this book is primarily an introduction to the general and basic elements of decentralised planning, I have accommodated both a theoretical perspective and the various points of view adopted by early and contemporary writers on decentralised planning.

The list of friends and colleagues who have collaborated with their opinions and comments is so long that it is impossible to thank them individually. However, I must specially mention my indebtedness to Rajat Choudhury, my Research Assistant and to Rajesh Jha. Rajesh, in spite of his busy schedule, tackled the manuscript with unflinching courage. Without him the book would not have emerged from the manuscript.

This book is dedicated to the many groups of officers and Panchayat functionarics who have participated in the various courses on decentralised planning at the Administrative Training Institute, Government of West Bengal, at Salt Lake. Their responses have greatly helped me in planning the content of the courses. In this sense, this book is indeed a participatory venture.

B.M. SANYAL

# CONTENTS

# 1

# HISTORY OF DECENTRALISED PLANNING IN INDIA

The concept of decentralised planning in this country is not of recent origin. In fact its antecedents can be traced back to the pre-independence days and the philosophy of Mahatma Gandhi. Mahatma Gandhi was an ardent advocate of small village-based communities which would be more or less self-sufficient. To make the dream of Gandhiji come true the Directive Principles of State Policy had commented in detail on the importance of village panchayats which are one of the principal institutions of a decentralised system of governance.

The Ripon Resolution of 1882 laid the foundation of modern local self-government institution in this country. It proposed the establishment of rural local boards for which non-official members would be elected. However, nominations in place of elections became the practice. Though the resolutions stated otherwise the district magistrates were made chairmen of these boards. The rural local boards started establishing elementary schools, dispensaries, constructing minor roads, etc. However, the work of these boards was not satisfactory in the final analysis. The Royal Commission on Decentralisation (1909) pointed out the inadequacy of funds and excessive official control as the prime reason for the unsatisfactory functioning of the boards. This Commission recommended ways for increasing the revenue of the boards. It also proposed setting up of Taluk boards and village panchayats. The years preceding independence saw these boards being dogged by myriad problems of reduced grants, inadequate resources, official control and domination by elites. The boards functioned very badly in many states and were on the verge of closing down. India became free and a new Constitution was adopted in 1950. The Directive Principles of State Policy commented in detail on the position of the village panchayats in the new situation. Furthermore, the division of power and functions enshrined in Article 246 read with the Seventh Schedule of the Constitution, made multi-level planning almost a necessity. Article 40 of the Constitution (Directive Principles of State Policy) states that the state should take steps to organise village panchayats and endow them with such powers and authority as may be necessary to enable them to function as units of self-government.

In accordance with the Directive Principles several states enacted legislation for establishing village panchayats. The Central Government helped the state governments in their task of strengthening the local self-government institutions. Conferences of state ministers dealing with local self-government were convened periodically by the Central Government for stock-taking and new suggestions towards strengthening these institutions were made. Though our early economic thinkers understood the importance of decentralised or multi-level planning set-up, they did not go into the details of operationalising the same. During the First Five-year Plan period experimental work on community development, in accordance with the ideas of decentralisation, was started with 'pilot project' on rural development of Mahela Block in Etawah district. The result of this project brought about the establishment of community development blocks. An infrastructure was also established which would facilitate coordination of developmental and administrative machinery. The community development blocks were assigned the task of developing clusters of villages. During the mid-fifties the planners emphasised the importance of people's participation in the planning process. This, according to them, could be achieved through democratic decentralisation with the district as the kingpin of the planning structure.

In 1957 the Planning Commission appointed a study team with Sri Balwant Rai Mehta as the chairman. The study team made an assessment of the functioning of the community development blocks and plan projects. In its report the Balwant Rai Mehta Committee noted, "So long as we do not discover or create a representative and democratic institution which will supply local interest, supervision and care necessary to ensure that expenditure of money upon local objects conforms to the needs and wishes of the locality, invest it with adequate power and assign to it appropriate finances, we will never be able to evoke local interest and excite local initiative in the field of development." The report submitted by the committee made a plea for decentralisation. It recommended establishing a three-tier local self-government institution which would enable decentralisation of administration and democratisation of power. The three tiers would be the panchayat at the village level, the *Panchayat Samiti* for a group of villages with executive powers and *Zilla Parishad* at the district level as the advisory body. The government accepted the recommendations and by 1963 legislations were framed by many states for establishing these panchayats.

The Panchayati Raj Institutions (PRIs) functioned reasonably well during the early sixties, but with the passage of time their functional efficiency began to deteriorate. The factors that contributed to this deterioration were lack of political will and bureaucratic initiative. In many states the elections to the panchayat bodies were either held irregularly or not held at all. Again the powers devolved on the panchayats by the state government were often taken away at the slightest pretext. The decisions taken by the PRI bodies were often overruled by politicians. It so happened that many of the newly introduced schemes were handed over for implementation to line departments which resulted in marginalisation of the PRI bodies. So decentralised planning, through the instrument of PRI, received a jolt.

During the Third Five-Year Plan period the concept of decentralisation was again resurrected in a big way. The Third Five-Year Plan specified that the states should formulate plans for areas like agriculture, minor irrigation, soil conservation, social forestry, animal husbandry, poultry and dairying, village industries, cooperatives, elementary education, etc. It was mentioned that such plans should be for district and block levels. But this kind of planning could not be initiated due to lack of necessary machinery.

The Fourth Five-Year Plan period is of some importance to the history of decentralised planning in this country. This plan put stress on district planning and noted that the district plan should be prepared in a more detailed way with added stress on setting up infrastructural facilities. However, the concept of 'integrated area approach' enjoyed popularity during this period. This entailed people's participation in the planning process and located appropriate socio-economic functions for particular places depending on their resource and other endowments. An attempt was made to relate state plans with physical features, resource endowments and institutional machinery of an area. The district planning concept was elaborated upon and discussed in detail. Methodologies were laid down. In accordance with the guidelines various states prepared district plans but the incorporation of the same in the annual plans did not materialise.

However, the area-specific beneficiary-oriented programmes that were taken up during this period have elevated the importance of the same as regards the history of decentralised planning in India. These programmes (namely CAB, DDP, SFDA and MFAL) were implemented by special agencies created for this purpose. However, these programmes were not in coordination with the district plans and their success was limited.

That all was not well with the planning mechanism of the country was being felt for sometime. Especially it was observed that inspite of so many years of planning, the benefits of economic growth had not reached the lower rungs of society. Need-specific programmes (20-point programme) and target-specific programmes were launched to make frontal attack on poverty. Also, in keeping with the philosophy of decentralisation, in this plan period, the block was decided to be the most appropriate level from where planning should start. A working group on block planning was set up in 1977 which strongly advocated block-level planning. It stressed on the fact that the planners at the district level, being situated too far away from the actual place where the plan is being implemented, have to face various problems which lead to improper allocation of funds and other related ills. The Planning Commission at this time issued guidelines for block-level planning.

The Ashok Mehta Committee (1977) was appointed to review the working of the Panchayati Raj Institutions and specially to demarcate the role of these representatives in the area of integrated rural development. The terms of reference of the committee enjoined upon it, among other things, to recommend the form and content of the relationship that should exist among the PRI, the official administrative machinery, and the cooperative and voluntary institutions involved in rural development.

The Committee identified a period of growth followed by a period of stagnation and finally one of decline for the Panchayati Raj.

1959-64 was identified as the period of growth, 1965-69 as the period of stagnation and finally 1969-77 as the period of decline. The Committee pointed out various factors that had adversely affected the functioning of the PRI and had made them ineffective (excepting in some states). The principal reason cited by the committee was the fact that although community development programme was put under the control of the PRI, several centrally sponsored schemes like SFDA, DPAP, etc. were not brought under the PRI's purview. Other problems like transfer of staff from PRI to various other departments engaged in development administration or the tendency of bureaucracy to work by organisational principles of line hierarchy further thwarted the working of PRI. The Ashok Mehta Committee commented, "... an overview of the national scene would indicate that the activities of the PRIs were meagre, their resource base weak and the overall attention given to them niggardly. The functioning of the Panchayati Raj system thus became discouraging. As if this was not enough, some of the state governments would postpone the holding of elections or supersede some of the important tiers of PRIs for one reason or the other. The lukewarm attitude of the political elite at higher levels towards strengthening of the democratic process at the grassroots level was generally the crux of the matter. In the ultimate analysis, all this led to a weakening of political support to PRIs and of the administrative will to work through them."

The Planning Commission appointed a working group (the Dantwala Committee - 1978) to shed light on how to go about experimenting with block-level planning. It was suggested by the committee that block-level planning was the appropriate tool for fighting rural poverty and implementing rural employment programmes. According to the Dantwala Committee a multi-disciplinary team of experts headed by a chief planning officer should form an important part of the district planning machinery and they should take part in block plan formulation as desired technical expertise is not available at the block level. Also the report said that state government could seek the assistance of universities and research institutions in drawing up the block plans. The committee stressed on the importance of reforming the agrarian structure and institutional set-up in the context of block-level planning. Structural changes, it said, were necessary at the social and economic levels so that exploitation of the poor could be decreased. Schemes that generate employment at the block-level should be taken up and these should have some bearing on intensification and/or diversification of agriculture and also promotion and/or rehabilitation of rural industries. One important thrust of the report was its assertion that block-level planning should not only concentrate on local development activities for asset creation and employment generation but should also be geared towards institutional reforms and organisation. It was suggested by the committee that initially 100 blocks should be chosen for block level planning which would gradually cover 500 blocks by the end of the plan period.

The Sixth Plan noted that though block planning was important for poverty alleviation, it was putting too much emphasis on the need for providing gainful employment. This transformed the block planning exercise to a kind of one-point programme, one that had the only goal of providing employment. This plan again switched back to district planning which was to be guided by "backlog-cum-problem oriented planning concept" and the "resource-cum-need based planning approach". The G.V.K. Rao Committee (1985) was appointed during the Sixth Plan period. It recommended a stress on *Zilla Parishad*. It advocated some transfer of planning functions to the district.

The working group (Hanumantha Rao Committee) found that "most of the states are at the beginning of the scale of decentralisation". The report of the working group dwelt at length on the actual state of affairs in the context of decentralised planning. It says, "... planning functions have not percolated to the district levels and only a limited job of assembling departmental schemes within the district frame is now being attempted." The report gave a clear account of how district planning is carried out in various states. It said, "...usually, after the state budget is voted in the assembly, the different heads of departments are requested to make a districtwise break-up of the outlays provided in the plan budget. This is then communicated to the districts either by sectoral departments or by the planning department of the state. This usually takes four to five months from the commencement of the financial year. After the communication is received, the district attempts to incorporate a write-up for the districtwise outlay and a document called 'district plan' emerges in this manner, which is purely an aggregation of departmental schemes. It should be noted that the choice of projects to be included in the sectoral outlays communicated to the districts in most states is a matter of state level initiative with district level support." The report of this working group brought out the sorry state of affairs of the decentralised planning system of this country. It observed, "So far as the panchayati raj institutions at the district level are concerned these have not been given the task of planning in any of the states, although many of the legislations in the states provide for this function."

The working group arrived at the conclusion that only a stepwise approval towards greater decentralisation through an *action-learning* process is possible in this country. The working group proposed three stages in this attempt towards total decentralisation by the year 2000 A.D. The first stage consists of putting up adequate planning machinery at the district level and breaking up of the state plans into district components. The second stage is the stage of 'limited decentralisation'. Herein a limited sector of activities like agriculture, target-group projects, minimum needs programme, etc. are brought under the fold of district-level planning and also the methods of allocation of funds between the state and district are worked out. The final stage will push localism to district sector decision making in all activities. Further in this stage all decision-making powers will be delegated to the district level through administrative reforms. The working group posited a district planning body which would be invested with all the planning activities in a multi-level planning framework of which the district planning exercise is a sub-system.

The importance of district level planning was reiterated by the Seventh Plan, though much progress in this direction was not seen during the plan's period of operation.

The L.M. Singhvi Committee (1986) was appointed during this time. It stressed on *Gram Sabha* as the seat of democracy. It further held that local self-government should be constitutionally recognised and regular elections to these should be held. During this time the government also appointed a commission popularly known as the Sarkaria Commission which was primarily set up to look into the existing arrangements of separation of powers between the centre and the states. Sarkaria Commission discussed in detail matters related to decentralised multi-level planning and strongly advocated participation of people's representatives for better planning and improved functions of the administrative machinery at the local level.

It recommended the creation of a body similar to finance commission at the state level which would facilitate devolution or transfer of resources to the districts.

The Eighth Five-Year Plan period is undoubtedly the most important period in the history of planning in India as far as decentralisation is concerned. It is during this period that decentralisation and the necessary processes facilitating the same got constitutional sanction. Previously district and sub-district level planning were carried out under executive orders or state acts. The 73rd and 74th Constitution Amendments have, however, brought a sea-change in the state of affairs. Without any constitutional sanction the decentralised planning process and organisations (like Panchayats) that were necessary for its smooth functioning were at the mercy of politicians. Elections to Panchayats were not held in many states and in quite a few instances decisions taken by these bodies were overruled. Also the lack of bureaucratic will severely restricted the panchayats' role as the most important player in a decentralised system.

A change in the situation is inevitable. The 73rd and 74th Amendments of the Constitution have made it mandatory for all states to hold elections for the panchayats within six months (in case of supression of any panchayat). So people's organisation, which is the best instrument for decentralised planning, has been sanctioned by the Constitution. As setting up of panchayats and the process of decentralisation have been given a constitutional status and is no more just a part of the Directive Principles these can no longer suffer from lack of political and bureaucratic will. Whether, the Panchayat would become another kind of bureaucracy and be plagued by bureaucratic diseases is a question that has been discussed elsewhere.

The salient features of these important amendments are :

(1) A fixed five-year tenure for Panchayats and compulsory elections to be held within six months in the event of suppression of any Panchayat.

(2) Disqualifications for membership of panchayats.

(3) Powers and responsibilities associated with preparation of plans for economic development and social justice have to

be devolved by the state legislature upon the panchayats. The specific items that have been handed over to the panchayats for planning are contained in the Eleventh Schedule (Article 243).

(4) Financial arrangements for the panchayats in the form of grants-in-aid authorised by the state legislature should be provided from the Consolidated Fund of the state. Also assignment to or appropriation by the panchayats of the revenues, duties, designated taxes, tolls and fees have to be made.

(5) Within a year of this amendment a State Finance Commission will be set up which will look into the financial condition of the panchayats and audit set-up after each 5-year period.

(6) Regarding Panchayat elections provisions should be made by the state legislature that the same may be held under the superintendence, direction and control of the Chief Electoral Officer of the state. Provisions of the said part will be applicable to the Union Territories; some states and areas have been excluded from the application of the provisions of the said part.

So it is clear that the 73rd and 74th Amendments of the Indian Constitution have provided a solid constitutional base for district and sub-district planning and are thereby furthering the goals of decentralisation. At last we reached a stage where very few hurdles (lack of political will, bureaucratic indifference, etc.) remain for the onward march of decentralisation and decentralised planning. In this context the following quote from Article 243 is important:

> "Subject to the provision of this Constitution, the Legislature of a state may, by law, endow the panchayats with such powers and authority as may be necessary to enable them to function as institutions of self-government and such laws may contain provisions for the devolution of powers and responsibilities upon panchayats at the appropriate level, subject to such conditions as may be specified therein with respect to,

(i) the preparation of plans for economic development and social justice;

(ii) the implementation of schemes for economic development and social justice as may be entrusted to them including those in relation to the matters listed in the Eleventh Schedule."

The reader may have often come across 'success stories' about the efficient panchayati raj operating in West Bengal and Karnataka and may get the idea that decentralised planning is being done smoothly in these places. However, this is not true. What we have in these states (and also in others) is horizontal decentralisation wherein the planning functions are divided among various departments corresponding to their areas of operation. These departmental plans are then bunched together to get the total plan for an area which will have a holistic focus. In this context inter-departmental coordination assumes great importance.

But there is still very little people's participation in the planning process. With the 73rd and 74th Amendments it is hoped that proper decentralisation will be achieved as people's organisations would be involved directly in plan formulation. A sense of belongingness would develop among these people at the grassroots level who will voice their needs and plan accordingly with assistance from the administration. But all this will be possible only if the panchayats do not get transformed into another slow-moving bureaucracy.

However, the Ashok Mehta Committee did not put down PRI as a total failure. It described the PRI with a note of admiration when it said, "Politically speaking, it became a process of democratic seed drilling in the Indian soil, making an average citizen more conscious of their rights than before. Administratively speaking, it bridged the gulf between the bureaucratic elite and the people. Socio-culturally speaking, it generated a new leadership which was not merely relatively young in age but also modernistic and pro-social change in outlook. Finally, from the developmental angle, it helped rural people cultivate a developmental psyche." The Committee directed its focus at the coordination of development activities below the state level and it suggested that the planning should start from the district. It was of the opinion that the requisite administrative and technical competence for planning was available at the district level only and not at some lower level. At the village level the primary planning unit should be a cluster of villages with a total population ranging from 10,000 to 15,000. According to the Committee, the planning body at the village level would be called *Mandal Panchayat*. So the district and the *Mandal Panchayat* will be the principal agencies responsible for decentralised planning according to the committee. The structure envisaged by the Ashok Mehta Committee is illustrated in the following quotation, "according to the structure that we envisage, the *Zilla Parishad* will be the first point of decentralisation of state developmental functions and it will take up planning for the district, coordinate the programmes and will guide the lower tiers. The *Panchayat Samiti* will basically be the executive committee of the *Zilla Parishad*, with such additional functions as may be assigned to it by the *Zilla Parishad*. The *Mandal Panchayat* will occupy a pivotal place in the scheme of *Panchayati Raj* being proposed by us. The place of the village set-up below the *Mandal Panchayat* will be analogous to that of the *Panchayat Samiti*. It will be an Executive Committee of the *Mandal Panchayat*, depending upon the size of the village concerned and local conditions." The report of the committee dwelt at length on the composition, elections and functions of the above bodies. It further elaborated on grassroots planning and the importance in looking after the interests of the weaker sections. A subsequent study (as we shall presently see) by the working group of the Planning Commission on district planning (1982), however, showed that there was hardly any decentralised planning in any of the states.

## Areas of Concern

If we consider decentralisation and the movement towards sustainable human development as an outcome of people's (India, in this case) instinct for survival then PRI is the child of this movement. A child on which much hope rests. However, the smooth and unhindered growth of PRI into a self-sustaining institution which will lead us towards the goal of sustainable human development is obstructed by many factors.

Principal among these is the juggernaut of the Indian bureaucracy whose role is primarily regulatory but of late developmental. Developmental functions have been by and by superimposed on the administrative machinery of our country giving rise to various conflicts. Due to certain historically inherited characteristics (of British vintage) the administrative structure is not amenable to a role of development planners and implementors. Moreover, it is actually antagonistic to the emergence of people's organisations and their role in plan formulation. For deep beneath the layers of red tape, service rules, acts, articles and code lies a fear of losing the power they have been enjoying for so long. This is because if people participate directly in planning, i.e., the PRI functions as units of self-government with both regulatory and developmental roles then the bureaucrats' power will be found waning.

What is necessary is cooperation and not conflict. PRIs and the administration have to work hand in hand if decentralised planning has to function smoothly in this country. The Participatory Rural Development (PRD) technique can be of much help in this regard by helping to establish a smooth and easy exchange of ideas between bureaucrats and people's representatives. PRD can also help in changing the negative stereotypes that each group has about the other.

But much in the administrative structure has to change. The present structure thwarts people's participation and thereby their all-round development. Apart from the basic unwillingness to relinquish its powers this is due to the lack of innovativeness, flexibility, expertise and accountablity of the bureaucracy. In place of proactive response the bureaucracy takes reactive measures dealing with the rural poor and their legitimate demands for equal rights and equal share of the fruits of progress.

The police service and the intelligence service are highly centralised structures and completely in contradiction to the federal structure found at the state level. In the name of national security and integrity these services function according to the whims of whoever is in command at the central or state level. The police and the intelligence services serve the functions of their colonial predecessors in their role of helping the state to increase its power and keep the rural poor in check. It would be better if they take up a new and challenging role as fomenting agents of development, a role where consensus gets precedence over conflict.

The administration of our country, in its role as an agent for change and development, is presently in the midst of a big crisis. It is facing organisational and management problems of a type and magnitude for which it has not been trained and prepared, especially in the face of increasingly militant demand for rights of the downtrodden. Penetrating analysis of the complexities and nuances of the present crisis is required for which well-grounded training in social sciences is necessary for the official administrative machinery, and the cooperative and voluntary institutions involved in rural development. However, the elite services like IPS, IAS, etc. lack such rigorous training in the social sciences and they work within a generalist frame of reference. Frequent transfers further undermine whatever personal initiative an officer of these cadres may have in dealing with the problems.

It is expected that the PRI will not remain another good idea that came to naught, but will, on the contrary, be a vibrant and useful organization instrumental (with the help of other well-thinking agencies) in giving the administrative system a new dimension and role as an agent of change for the better.

# 2

# CONCEPT OF DECENTRALISATION

Decentralisation, in simple terms, implies a movement away from the centre. But this is a truism and this concept needs further elucidation. It can be defined as an even distribution of power (in any or all of many forms) among all agents in the social, political and economic spheres. Such a process has many advantages and is supposed to strengthen democracy by involving independent groups like trade unions, farmers' organisations, consumer groups, various other elements of civil society and also people from the grassroots level. Decentralisation facilitates the articulation of people's needs and demands. Thus through decentralisation a state moves towards the avowed goals of development, principal among which is an addition to the entitlements of the deprived.

Decentralised governance, from capital cities to towns and villages, is the best way to involve people in development activities and for increasing efficiency. Local officials and politicians will be better scrutinised and their activities better monitored. They will be more accountable to the communities which they are supposed to serve. Decentralisation, by empowering the people from the grass-roots level, helps to generate a sense of belongingness among them and they get more deeply involved in developmental works.

Decentralisation can be of two types: *horizontal* and *vertical.* Horizontal decentralisation, which is more prevalent in this country, disperses power (e.g., the finance minister delegates some financial powers to different line departments but ultimate authority and power lies with the ministry itself) among institutions at the same level. On the other hand, vertical decentralisation, which is more important and necessary, allows some of the central government powers to be delegated downwards to lower and lower tiers of authority. Vertical decentralisation can be of four types.

1. *Deconcentration*

Passing down of administrative discretion to local authorities in a system where few decisions can be without reference to the central authority is called deconcentration. It results in some dispersal of power.

Actually deconcentration entails some shifting of workload in the form of administrative responsibilities from central offices of the executive to regional offices. Yet this does not give these latter offices discretionary freedom or the power to take decisions. Here authority and powers of central offices remain with the centre. Therefore deconcentration is also called *geographic decentralisation* or *administrative decentralisation*.

2. *Delegation*

If the central authority retains the right to overrule decisions of the local authority while giving it the right to exercise some authority and decision-making powers then such a form of decentralisation is called delegation. Moreover, in such a system the central authority can take away the powers of the local authority at any point of time.

3. *Devolution*

Devolution is the most desirable form of decentralisation. It grants decision making powers to local authorities and gives them the freedom to take full responsibility without referring back to the central authority. The devolved powers include financial powers and authority to design and execute projects and programmes. In case of devolution the local levels of government are allowed to act in a more or less autonomous fashion with the centre taking a supervisory role.

4. *Privatisation*

These apart there is yet another kind of decentralisation wherein the government hands over some of its responsibilities and public functions to private, non-governmental or voluntary organisations. Such voluntary organisations could be industrial associations, professional groups, cooperatives and the like. Similarly, totally private controlled enterprises can be handed over certain responsibilities and public functions. Decentralisation of this type is called privatisation.

When a government privatises PSUs by relinquishing all controls (financial, administrative, etc.) over such organisations then this act can be said to be an example of the fourth form of decentralisation discussed above. As there exist very few statistical measures for many aspects of decentralisation it is very difficult to quantify the extent of decentralisation in a particular country. Moreover, reliable data is very difficult to come by and in most cases the necessary data does not exist. While making cross-national comparisons of the degree of decentralisation we should keep in mind the fact that the priority accorded to decentralisation varies with the size of the country. Generally, decentralisation is of more importance to larger countries as compared to smaller ones. So the degree of decentralisation acceptable for one country may not be suitable for another. Again a government might apparently be very committed to the idea of decentralisation (of expenditure, say) but at the same time it may be retaining tight control over standards and priorities. In such a case decentralisation is meaningless. So when dealing with the various measures of decentralisation we should be careful not to be misled. The figures and ratios should always be complemented by a wider knowledge of the situation, the intricacies of governance and various systems that are followed in the concerned country.

Proper allocation and timely availability of funds for grass-roots level workers are the fulcrum of a decentralised planning infrastructure. Keeping this in mind we can define certain ratios that may be used for measuring financial decentralisation. These are :

1. *The expenditure decentralisation ratio:* It is the percentage share of the local government's expenditure in the total expenditure of the central government.

   The expenditure decentralisation ratio is in a way imperfect because it does not take into account the fact that there are some government expenditures (like defence, debt servicing, etc.) which by their nature have to be undertaken by the central government.

2. *The modified expenditure decentralisation ratio* : When the part of expenditure that cannot be decentralised is subtracted from the total government expenditure then the percentage of that remaining expenditure spent by the local government is called the modified expenditure decentralisation ratio. This ratio, to a great extent, reduces the drawbacks of the expenditure decentralisation ratio. Therefore it is called *modified.*

3. *The revenue decentralisation ratio* : This ratio measures the extent of the local government's liberties in generating revenue. It is the percentage share of local government revenue in total government revenue.

4. *The financial autonomy ratio* : It is a measure of the local government's independence from central government funding. It is the percentage share of revenue that is raised locally in the total local expenditure.

Again the control of social spending can be used as an indicator of decentralisation. This is so because it is generally presumed that when local governments are in charge of education or health (for instance) the resources are used more efficiently and there is more equitable distribution of benefits and better management. Moreover, the local government is expected to be more sensitive as far as the needs of the local communities are concerned.

To measure the distribution of social spending and thus get an idea about the extent and nature of decentralisation the following ratios may be used :

(1) *The central government social allocation ratio* : The social spending component expressed as percentage of the central government budget gives this ratio.

(2) *The local government social allocation ratio* : It is the social spending component expressed as a percentage of the local government budgets.

(3) *The social expenditure decentralisation ratio :* It is the ratio of local government social spending in the total social spending by the central government. It gives a measure of the extent of decentralisation in social spending.

# 3

# CONCEPT OF DECENTRALISED PLANNING

Having discussed the concept of decentralisation we need to know about decentralised planning and its conceptual framework as found in India. Decentralised planning is actually planning at different levels. This could imply planning for national level, state level, district level, block level, panchayat level, etc. Again this kind of planning could be for a particular region with agro-climatically homogeneous features.

Decentralised planning is really a multi-level planning and not a totally bottom-up kind of planning. It does not profess total replacement of centralised planning. It is a two-way planning process starting from the top (national) and the bottom (local level) simultaneously. The two processes merge with each other at a level below which centralised planning becomes irrelevant and unmanageable and above which micro-planning is not possible.

Macro, meso and micro levels of planning can correspond roughly to the national, state and district levels respectively.

Three important characteristics of planning in India are :

(1) The process operates under a democratic framework with elected governments at the centre and the state.

(2) The planning process operates through a system of federation where concurrent planning is involved.

(3) The planning process operates in a market-friendly economy.

## Objectives of Decentralised Planning

The prime objective of decentralised planning is the growth and distributive justice of the whole economy by suitably linking up local needs and priorities with avowed goals of development. The centralised planning we have been following till date has failed in various respects to deliver the goods. Though the values of some macro-indicators like GNP, agriculture/industrial production, etc. may have increased over the years the picture at the grassroots level is not exactly rosy. This is so because growth has not been accompanied by distributive justice. This is further underlined by the fact that a good percentage of our population is below the poverty line and the rate of unemployment has not shown any marked change. During the era of centralised planning emphasis had been on projects involving huge investments. Heavy industries, major and medium irrigations and other such areas were promoted. Thus the beneficiaries of the planning exercise were mainly the industrialists and big businessmen of urban areas and the better-off big farmers of the rural areas. The poorer sections of the population reaped little or no benefits from the planning process.

During the Fourth Five-Year Plan the issue of this imbalance and its remedy was raised for the first time. The same plan debated the appropriate planning unit for correcting imbalances and came to the conclusion that the district was the optimum unit for micro-level planning. But district-level planning was not much of a success as the ensuing years showed. It was understood that a smaller area would be more effective for obtaining desired results from micro-planning. This became clear when the problems of mobilising local material, human resources and managing agricultural activities, minor irrigation, rural industries, health, education, from such a large frame of reference became apparent. So community development blocks were chosen as appropriate planning units.

Block-level planning promised many things. First of all it did away with the possibility of duplication and redundancy which arises when sectoral plans are implemented in isolation. It was also a movement in the direction of decentralisation which the government had initiated. The system (of planning) that is still prevalent in this country depends much on the functioning of the local administration which is, however, detached from the people and answerable only to their superiors. Moreover, the group of administrators and the group of villagers have negative stereotypes about each other in their mind. This further complicates the problem and makes the case for decentralised, people-centred planning stronger. So what is required is a decentralised, people-centred, people's plan where involvement of the people is a *sine qua non*. In such a planning system plan formulation and implementation will be done by the people working side by side in harmony with administrative personnel. This will ensure that the benefits of planning reach the lowest rungs of society and the needs of the people are reflected in the executed projects. Again the geographical and agro-climatic disparities among regions have a reflection on the life of the people which necessitates decentralised planning to better their lot. This is so because the wide focus of centralised planning cannot take into account reasonably such disparities and make necessary adjustments.

# 4

# OBJECTIVES AND STRATEGIES OF DECENTRALISED PLANNING

## Objectives

The concept of decentralised planning that has been described can well be translated into certain objectives of decentralised planning. In framing such objectives we should, however, be amenable to change and act with judgement and discretion so that our actions are according to the needs of the local situation.

The broad objectives of decentralised planning can be divided into two categories, economic and social.

### *Economic Objectives*

(1) Employment opportunities must be provided to each and every able member of the community including the poorest of the poor. Poverty has to be removed.

(2) The local resources and the means of production should be gradually brought under the control of the local community so that true equality may be achieved.

(3) Local resources (material and human) should be used in combination with external inputs if the necessity arises.

(4) The production process should primarily be aimed at meeting the basic needs of the people. Whenever, any surplus is generated in the process this should go towards capital formation leading to development. The production process should be geared to maximise output with limited input of resources.

(5) The state plan goals should be met.

(6) Sustainable development should be achieved.

(7) There should be no duplication of work and there should be an effective inter-departmental coordination.

(8) Infrastructural facilities should be set up. This may include roads, warehouses, markets, power sources, distribution centres, cooperatives, etc.

*Social Objectives*

(1) The plan should try to do away with exploitation and injustice.

(2) It should be designed in a way that people's participation is fostered so that they may develop a sense of belongingness and become self-reliant.

(3) Local needs and aspirations should be reflected in the plan.

(4) It should aim at removing disparities (in many forms).

(5) Fellow feeling and mutual help should be promoted through the plan and various groups should feel motivated to take up developmental tasks.

## Strategies

The objectives (discussed earlier) and the strategies of decentralised planning to be discussed here are to be kept in mind while formulating the decentralised people-centred plan. The strategies are like building blocks or broad guidelines to be followed while going into the nitty-gritties of the actual planning process.

A decentralised planning strategy should give proper importance to the needs of the people and the local potentials and drawbacks while aiming at the goal of sustainable development. It should aim at optimising utilisation of local resources after prior assessment of development potentials. Feasible projects should be designed for the thrust areas that are identified while the functional and spatial aspects of resource development should be taken care of. This will foster all-round growth. Again the needs of the people and agro-climatic peculiarities of a region should be properly assessed and should be reflected in the plan. However, for achieving greater equality there should be a bias towards areas which are socio-economically deprived or areas in which there is a scarcity of resources. Rural growth centres have to be identified and the planning machinery should concentrate on these areas so that urban and rural disparties are minimised and a rural-urban continuum is developed. This will further prevent rural-urban migration and reduce the pressure on agriculture. As mentioned in the objectives of decentralised planning the bridging of gaps in socio-economic infrastructure should be given utmost importance. The fund flow for plan implementation has to be assessed and well managed. Multi-sectoral projects have to be properly phased and most importantly, appropriate monitoring and evaluation systems have to be set up so that the cherished goals of development are realised. The credit plans of banks and financial institutions have to be linked up with the district plan. Last but not the least, the plan should include mechanisms that allow greater degree of people's participation in the monitoring and evaluation stages of the various programmes.

# 5

# PARTICIPATORY RURAL DEVELOPMENT-A TECHNIQUE OF INVOLVING PEOPLE IN DECENTRALISED PLANNING PROCESS

The basic objective of planning is the optimum use of scarce resources for sustainable development. All of us want development but if limitless craving for goods becomes the engine of development, the concept of sustainable development is vitiated. When we have a quest for more and more goods and services and that too in better quality, we are headed for mindless consumerism. This thirst to fulfil material desíre blurs our vision of true development. True development is surely an expansion of human capabilities, that is, integrated development of man. Development will surely bring more and better bundle of goods and services for man, but apart from that, development should also create enabling environment for man to attain his/her inner development. This is very crucial for holistic development. If development negates the ethical and moral part and only highlights the growth aspect, that is, more and more production of goods and services, the purpose of development will be self-defeating. This materialistic development will create selfish giants among men devoid of any altruistic spirit which is the touchstone of any sustainable development. The concept of sustainable development as it is manifested by economy, ecology and equity is a value-based development concept while conventional development theory of the West—development trajectory as represented by Harrod-Domar or Rostow's stages of economic growth—measures development either in terms of physical growth or rate of high mass consumption; consumerism as the be all and end all of economic development devoid of any ethical and moral value. If some physical bundle of goods and services becomes the centre stage of development where everybody does not have equal access, that will lead to deprivation of millions for the betterment of few. Here we face the ends and means problem. We are talking about planning for development but such planning should be people-oriented. Development is the means to an end. The end is improvement in the quality of human life. Hence, the centre stage of development should be people for whom we plan. This can happen when planning becomes participatory.

When government plans for the country, such planning is also participatory in the sense that people take part in the development process, but this is passive participation. In a parliamentary democracy people participate in the administration indirectly, that is, through the elected representatives of the people. Once elected by simple majority the elected leader virtually rules over the entire electorate unlike the Greek city state where everybody belongs to the decision-making process and no one is left out. True participatory planning is said to occur when the plan is framed at the grassroots level. From formulation stage to implementing and monitoring stage people have to play a decisive role. Only people-centred plan can be truly participatory. In a country like India with almost 96 crores of people and millions of villages, only the functioning of grassroots level institutions like panchayat system can enable us to draw a participatory plan. PRI at the grassroots level is the only people's organisation which can well understand the stress on the carrying capacity of the fragile eco-system of the particular region representing a typical agro-climatic zone. The basic thrust of decentralised planning is to draw up micro-plans. For this resources have to be accounted locally and PRI is the only locally sustainable organisation which can take cognizance of these factors to draw up an environmentally sound plan, with effective community participation in decision making. An effective panchayat can create better consciousness about unsustainable practices among the villagers consisting of various heterogeneous groups of development stake holders within the community. People-friendly Panchayat can draw up a sustainable micro-plan reflecting harmonious development of the area taking into account bio-diversity at the local level.

**Decentralised Planning and the Participatory Plan**

The dencentralised planning process involves a combination of the top down and bottom up approach to planning. Under the decentralised planning framework the panchayat bodies and the district administration are supposed to cooperate with each other so that a comprehensive plan from the grassroots level can emerge. In this context it is important to mention that with the 73rd and 74th Amendments of the Constitution the Panchayat Raj Institution has been made mandatory throughout the country and panchayats have been given wide powers in the implementation and formulation of the plan.

Most important is the prioritisation of needs of the grassroots level people, through the use of PRD method (described later). This is where the role of Panchayat assumes great importance because being in touch with the people it can facilitate the smooth progress of the PRD exercise.

The PRI comprises three elected bodies of *Zilla Parishad* (district level), *Panchayat Samiti* (block level) and *Gram Panchayat* (village level). At each of these levels the needs of the people are appraised by the relevant panchayat bodies and prioritization is done with the help of the corresponding administrative personnel. PRD methods can be used to much benefit during these prioritisation steps and the administrative bodies can work side by side with the panchayats during the use of PRD techniques. The emerging priorities should be compatible with the ideas of sustainable development which is one of the focuses of decentralised planning. The use of PRD exercise during prioritisation will help to generate whole hearted participation from the grassroots level. This is so because the panchayat which will play an important role during the use of PRD, being in direct contact with the people will be able to develop a sense of belongingness and motivation among them. The PRD technique will be most fruitfully used if an inter-disciplinary team consisting of members of various departments is involved in the exercise. The prioritisation process will be facilitated by the combined use of specialised knowledge of different departmental personnel, district administration and panchayat body members.

However, the process of prioritisation and development of a sense of belongingness will give best results if two non-elected panchayat bodies comprising all electors at the village level (namely *Gram Sabha* and *Gram Samsad*) are utilised. These non-elected bodies being free from the negative influences of bad politics can best understand the needs of the people. Also being composed of all electors these bodies are best informed about the prevailing situation at the grassroots level.

The final set of priorities that emanates from the Panchayat Samiti (block level panchayat body) in the form of an ex-ante plan is to be sent to the *Zilla Parishad* which starts identifying appropriate projects to meet the priorities that are submitted in the form of a block plan. The available resources (budget) collected from various sources is a vital determinant in the process of project identification at the district level. If the total demand for funds (from various identified projects) is more than the supply then some of the projects have to be shelved for the time being. Identification of projects would be based on consideration of various important points like availability of inputs, available technological possibilities, marketing and other support, etc.

Once the projects that will be implemented to meet the prioritised needs have been identified subject to the various constraints (like fund availability, technological option, etc.) we can say that the district plan is ready.

The ex-post or realised block plan will then be implemented according to the projects that have been finally selected by the district subject to the previously mentioned constraints and also the district level priorities. This final selection of projects at district level is done by the *Zilla Parishad* with the assistance of the district administration at the District Planning Committee (DPC) level. The *Zilla Parishad* being an elected panchayat body, political will, political favours and conflicts play an important role in the final selection of projects.

Next the identification of responsibilities begins. Identification of responsibilities in project implementation is of utmost necessity for the smooth and successful progress of project work. Alongwith this the documentation process starts so that a record of progress and failure can be kept.

With the experience gathered during implemention (which is amply documented) the existing database is updated and this helps in formulation of future plans.

## THE PRD METHODOLOGY

Participatory Rural Development (PRD) is a methodology of involving rural people in the solution of their own problems. This technique combines various tools of management and psychoanalysis and aims at developing a sense of belongingness and trust among the rural people. PRD incorporates the techniques of Participatory Rural Appraisal (Robert Chambers), Action Learning (Revans), and Transactional Analysis (Eric Berne).

### Participatory Rural Appraisal (PRA)

The Participatory Rural Appraisal (PRA) method is an important constituent of PRD. PRA is a methodology adopted with the intention of systematically securing the active participation and involvement of the rural community in activities meant for their benefit. It ensures proper implementation of carefully thought-out measures which are executed with the help and cooperation of the community and continued and regulated by it.

A comparison of the PRA method and the Questionnaire Research Method (QRM) will clearly bring out the advantages and drawbacks of each. The PRA approach needs less time, involves low cost and is a very flexible method as against the QRM which involves more time, high cost and is not flexible. Again the PRA approach involves high participation and little statistical analysis depending more on on-the-spot analysis, whereas QRM involves low participation and heavy statistical analysis in the office. Semi-structured interviews and group discussions form an integral part of the PRA method as opposed to the use of formal questionnaire in QRM. A multi-disciplinary team is necessary for using the PRA method and they work with an opportunity sample while in QRM enumerators work with random sample. PRA method is best for learning and understanding rural people's opinions, behaviours and attitudes while QRM is useful for gathering representative quantitative data followed by statistical analysis.

So PRA is an intensive, systematic but semi-structured learning experience in a community by a multi-disciplinary team and community members. It can be used in assessment of needs or for feasibility studies. Again it helps in identifying priorities for development activities and monitoring and evaluation of the same. The basic purpose of PRA is to gain an understanding of the complexities of a topic rather than to gather highly accurate statistics on a list of variables. It is also aimed at learning the attitude and opinions of community members which implies that what majority of the people tell must be taken into consideration.

The manifest strengths of the PRA method are due to certain remarkable features that it possesses :

(1) The PRA technique helps the rural community to take initiative and share the responsibilities of their upliftment perfectly realising the importance of such communities in the development process.

(2) The concept of participatory action is ingrained in the PRA approach as it brings together the intended beneficiaries and the planners on a common platform. Also different interest groups within the community get equal chance to participate.

(3) PRA uses methods of communication which are easily intelligible to the rural people obviating the necessity of lengthy interaction. Such methods include the use of visual materials like maps, sketches, etc. which have a greater impact than any formal method.

4) PRA develops a sense of belongingness among the people who as a result begin to associate themselves with their problems. Prioritisation of needs and subsequent planning can naturally follow PRA.

(5) Different sectors can be integrated and appraised together with the help of PRA technique.

(6) PRA acts as an interface between people from the grassroots level and the developmental organisations and the government. It puts stress on collaborative means like discussions, deliberations to promote constructive joint action unhindered by bureaucratisation, artificial compartmentalisation and other such ills.

This brings us to the next important section in this discussion on PRA. This section concerns the actual techniques that have to be used in a PRA exercise. Before doing that we will briefly underline the attitude on the part of planners that are to be cultivated to make the PRA exercise successful.

**Attitudes Favouring PRA**

(1) *Participation* : A participatory approach is absolutely essential. All villagers should be made to feel that they are indispensable for the success of the programme and they should not feel alienated.

(2) *Respect for community members* : The planners taking part in the exercise should show equal respect to all members of the community.

(3) *Eagerness to learn and listen* : While doing a PRA exercise the planners should cultivate the attitude of learners. That is, they should be eager to listen and abstain from lecturing. A whole-hearted interest in what village people know, say and do is absolutely necessary for the success of PRA.

(4) *Humility and patience* : Instead of thinking themselves to be in any way superior to the villagers the planners should evince humility and patience. They should not rush through the various steps of the exercise.

(5) *Willingness to empower villagers* : The planners should be willing to use methods which empower the villagers such that they share, enhance and analyse their knowledge.

The actual use of PRA technique is based on the use of various tools and its planning and implementation stage involve:

(1) *Selection and Sensitisation of PRA Team Members*

This is a crucial step on which the success or failure of the PRA exercise depends. The PRA team members should have intuition, empathy and perceptive power and moreover, they should be good practical communicators (in the language of the villagers). An ideal member for a PRA team must be unobstrusive, respectful, sensitive, possessing a good memory, having good writing skills, a good listener, engaging and open. Males and females as well as people from different castes and religions should be represented in the PRA team. An ideal appraiser should be conversant with the culture of the people among whom the PRA exercise is to be undertaken.

Following the selection of the PRA team members, an orientation and guidance programme should provide unambiguous guidelines regarding the roles of the team members and the goals of the PRA exercise. The team members should be so oriented that (a) they are able to write descriptively and accurately, (b) they can separate useful information from non-essentials, (c) they can avoid prejudices as to the desired nature of responses, (d) they can keep a detailed and organised note on field activities. Gender sensitisations should also form an important part of the orientation programme. Last but not the least, the PRA team should be made aware during orientation about the uniqueness, specialities, etc. of the area and the people they will be interacting with.

### (2) *Site Selection*

The selection of an appropriate site where the PRA exercise is to be undertaken is one of the important steps of the exercise. In the context of formulating agro-climatically homogeneous region based plans for this country (an idea envisaged and presently being promoted by the Planning Commission) the PRA exercise and its success depends much on the active participation and cooperation of the panchayat system (made mandatory through the 73rd and 74th Constitution Amendments). The Panchayati Raj Institution and its members being directly in touch with people from the grassroots level can be of immense help during site selection and other later stages of the PRA exercise. As panchayat members are aware of conditions prevailing at the grassroots level they can assist in these various steps of the PRA exercise.

### (3) *Community Preparation*

This stage involves informing the villagers and preparing them for the visit by the PRA team. Community preparation is facilitated by the panchayat. As the panachayat members have direct links with people from the grassroots level they can easily interact and communicate with them thus preparing them for the visit by the PRA team.

(4) *Materials and Logistical Support*

Materials in the form of colour pens, pencils, sticks, stones, *rangoli,* chalk paper etc. are necessary for preparing maps and charts during the PRA exercise. Logistical support can be given by resource persons from NGOs and panchayat members who can guide the smooth progress of the PRA exercise.

(5) *Schedules*

Wealth ranking, matrix ranking, seasonality-of-employment diagrams and other schedules, charts, etc. are prepared during the PRA exercise to get an idea of the prevailing situation of the area under consideration.

(6) *Process Documentation*

Documentation of the PRA exercise can be of many forms. The whole process can be taperecordered or videographed. Again, still photographs can be taken of the maps, charts, etc. prepared by the villagers as also of various moods and moments of the process. Moreover, a detailed report can be prepared on the total PRA exercise. This may take the form of a minute by minute account or it could be a general report on the exercise. Anyone or all these forms of process documentation can be used for recording the PRA exercise.

Various tools that can be used during the PRA exercise are enumerated below followed by description of the methodology of using a few of these :

**PRA Tools**

There are many techniques that can be useful in a PRA exercise. However, which among these can be used and whether they should be used individually or in combination depends upon various factors like available time, available resources and the desired results.

These tools are :

(1) Direct observation (observation indicator check lists)
(2) Preference ranking and scoring
(3) Focus group discussion
(4) Analysis group discussion
(5) Ranking by voting
(6) Direct matrix ranking
(7) Wealth ranking
(8) Partwise ranking and scoring
(9) Semi-structured interview
(10) Secondary data review
(11) Innovation assessment
(12) Construction of diagrams
(13) Mapping and modelling
(14) Social mapping
(15) Historical and future (vision) mapping
(16) Mobility mapping
(17) Participatory mapping
(18) Transect diagrams
(19) Transect walks
(20) Historical transect
(21) Seasonal calendar
(22) Historical seasonal calendar
(23) Time trends
(24) Historical profile
(25) Livelihood analysis
(26) Pie charts
(27) Participant observation (do-it-yourself, learning by doing)
(28) Venn/Institutional Diagram
(29) Thipparpur method : an alternative to Venn diagramming

(30) Flow/Causal diagram

(31) System diagram

(32) Histogram

(33) Oral histories

(34) Workshop and workshopping

(35) Group walks

(36) Stories

(37) Folklore

(38) Case studies and portraits

(39) Indigenous categories and terms, taxonomies and ethno-classification

(40) Triangulation

A brief outline regarding participatory mapping, transects seasonal calendar and triangulation is given below :

**Participatory Mapping**

The first step of participatory mapping concerns the decision regarding the sort of map that is to be prepared. The map could be of village residential area (social), village land area (natural resources), watershed, forests and farms, etc. Participatory mapping helps to develop a sense of involvement among the villagers which will later motivate them to come forward for solving their own problems.

Next, the PRA team will have to find people among the villagers who are willing to share their knowledge. The Local Panchayat body members can come forward and help the PRA team because they (Panchayat body members) are in direct contact with the people at the grassroots level.

Following this, a suitable place where the map would be drawn and a suitable medium will have to be chosen. The bare ground, floor or any flat surface or paper can be used for map drawing. Sticks, stones, rangoli, chalks, pencils, colour pens, etc. can be used to prepare the maps.

The village people should get started themselves in the map drawing process with the PRA team members acting as facilitators. A permanent record of the map with names of the persons who draw it should be kept.

In this context it has to be mentioned that instead of a single map a succession of maps drawn by the villagers is more effective as it acts as a boost to the process of involvement. From the map drawing exercise the process should move on to the preparation of transects, wealth ranking, topical PRA, etc.

## Transect

A transect is a diagram showing the main land use zones of the area under consideration. It is used to compare the resources, main features, and the problems and opportunities of different zones.

To draw a transect first of all knowledgeable community members should be assembled who are willing to participate in a walk through their village and surrounding areas. Then the PRA team should discuss with the villagers the different factors that have to be covered by the transect (crops, landuse, trees, soil, etc.) as also the route to be taken. The group comprising team members and villagers should then walk the transect and discuss problems and opportunities. During this time they should abstain from lecturing and only observe, ask and listen. After drawing the transect it should be cross-checked with key informants.

## Seasonal Calendar

A seasonal calendar is a diagrammatic form of representation which portrays activities, problems and opportunities throughout the annual cycle. It helps to identify important variances during the period under consideration, such as the month when employment opportunities are minimum.

## Triangulation

Triangulation is a method of purposefully looking at the same problems from different viewpoints and formulating different solutions based on these varied approaches. It helps to cross-check information and thus enables elicitation of accurate information.

Having completed our elaboration on some of the more important PRA techniques we will now be discussing some dangers, limitations and difficulties of using PRA. Thus we will be able to get an idea of the drawbacks of this technique and will be able to move on to the other techniques which may be used to compliment PRA and increase its effectiveness. PRA in combination with these other techniques will constitute the methodology of PRD which has been mentioned earlier.

**Limitations, Dangers and Difficulties of PRA Implementation**

(1) Statistical surveys, long-term anthropological studies and such other methods need to be used together with PRA for best results. However, the PRA technique does not claim to dislodge other research methods from their application contexts and does not pose as a universal methodology suitable for all situations.

(2) The use of PRA techniques may raise local expectations. This, however, has a positive fall-out. It increases the importance, and hopefully, the motivation for initiating follow-up action.

(3) PRA methods are not universal in nature, which means that they have to be modified and adapted according to local conditions.

(4) Proper training of the facilitators and participants is of utmost importance for the success of PRA.

(5) The PRA technique allows the team members (planners) to see only a part of the whole situation denying them the facility of viewing the total picture.

(6) PRA loses its importance if there is no need for involving the people.

(7) Sensitive issues like caste conflicts, gender dominance, etc. cannot be discussed while using PRA techniques.

(8) There exists the danger in PRA of being misled by myth, gossip and folklore.

(9) Rural women generally do not participate whole-heartedly in the PRA exercise. This aloofness stems from inferiority complex of women which has been formed and fostered by gender biases. However, there are exceptions. Women in tribal areas are often highly motivated. Again, if the PRA team has female members then they can help in motivating the womenfolk. So it is desirable that female members be a part of the PRA team.

(10)The tendency of the PRA team members to lecture instead of listening and learning and the lack of humility and respect (for the villagers and their opinions) on their part may seriously hamper the PRA implementation exercise.

## TRANSACTION ANALYSIS

The tools of PRA can be used in the village only after an amicable atmosphere conducive to conversation and discussion has been built up. The villagers are usually bogged down by various customs, traditions, beliefs, etc. and they will not easily come forward to talk with the PRA team members. To make PRD a success its methodology incorporates some techniques other than PRA which will supplement PRA and pave the way for its smooth execution. One such indispensable technique which has to be used before commencement and also during the PRA exercise is the technique of Transactional Analysis (TA).

Transactional Analysis is a useful tool which helps people better understand themselves and other individuals. It has widespread applications in management and other behavioural sciences. In our context TA is of immense help and use for the successful execution of PRD programmes which later facilitate micro-level planning.

Transactional Analysis is a method of examining and analysing communication among individuals by breaking such communication into the basic unit of social intercourse called *transaction*. Eric Berne defined this basic unit of social intercourse thus : "When two or more persons come across each other sooner or later one of them will speak or give some indication acknowledging the presence of others. Such acknowledgement, whatever form it might take, is called transactional stimulus. Another person will then say or do something which is somehow related to the initial transactional stimulus. This response by the other person has been called transactional response."

## Ego-states and the PAC Model

By observing people Berne came to the conclusion that each individual comprises three different ego-states, namely the Parent (P), the Adult (A) and the Child (C). People generally exhibit all three ego-states but one state may dominate the other two. It is believed that the adult ego-state is far superior to the other two states, at least for effective inter-personal relations, TA theorists hold that all three ego-states are necessary for a healthy personality. The ego-states are not in the nature of roles but are rather psychological realities, coherent systems of thought and feeling manifested by corresponding patterns of behaviour.

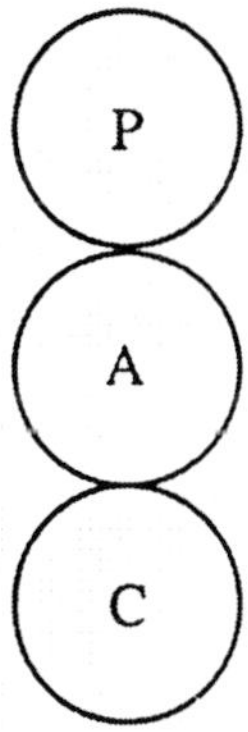


Structural Diagram

## Parent Ego-state

The parent ego-state results from the incorporation of the attitudes and behaviour of all significant people who serve as parent figures to the child. Thus it (parent ego-state) involves an attitude of value sharing, sharing of beliefs, norms, prejudices and traditions. The parent state comprises a huge collection of recordings in the brain of unquestioned or imposed events experienced by a person in his early years. This collection of recordings is specific for every person. In this state people act like parents and parental figures. Parent ego-state can be divided into *nurturing parent* (overly protective and loving) and *critical parent* (critical and stern). In the parent ego-state individuals tend to treat others like children and talk down to people. Physical clues to identify the parent ego-state includes furrowed brow, pursed lips, the 'horrified look', arms folded across chest etc. In the parent ego-state individuals tend to use words like stupid, nonsense, ridiculous, etc., and sentences beginning with 'now always remember....', 'If I were you....', etc.

### The Adult Ego-state

An adult ego-state involves sharing of facts and information without influence of emotion and value. In this state people objectively appraise their environment and calculate its probabilities and possibilities on the basis of information received and with the support of available data. In the adult-ego state a person is cool headed, rational and as such can process and analyse information objectively and carefully and make logical conclusions. Instead of being domineering, impulsive and overbearing an adult ego-state is characterised by fairness and objectivity. The adult is like a data processing computer which takes decisions after computing the information from the parent, the child and the data which are already in the adult from ongoing experience. The adult examines the data in the parent, sees whether or not it is true and still applicable today and then accepts or rejects it. It also examines the feelings in the child, sees if they are appropriate to the present or not. Physical clues to identify the adult ego-state include continual movement of the face, eyes, body, with an eye blinking every three to five seconds when he is listening. The words often used in the adult ego-state include 'why', 'what', 'where', etc. and sentences he would be using will be of the form, "It is my opinion that..." or 'I think that....', etc.

### Child Ego-state

A person in the child ego-state is emotional, instinctive and impulsive.

The child ego-state consists of all urges and feelings that come naturally to the individual. Different impulses and feelings are expressed at different ages. Therefore, when a person is in the grip of this feeling, we say his child has taken over; when his anger dominates his reason we say his child is in command. The child also consists of a recording of his early feelings and how he reacted to them. The child ego-state contains within itself creativity, curiosity, the desire to explore and know, the urges to touch and feel and experience and the recording of the glorious, pristine feeling of first discoveries.

The child ego-state can be better understood through its subdivisions: natural child/free child, little professor/creative child and adapted child as illustrated in the functional diagram below.

The natural child expresses himself spontaneously without concern for the reaction of parents or the world.

Adapted child always tries to conform to authority and pleases those on whom it is dependent. The adapted child is expressed when the individual uses automatic patterns of behaviour which enable him to get along with, and get some kind of attention from the "big people" in his life.

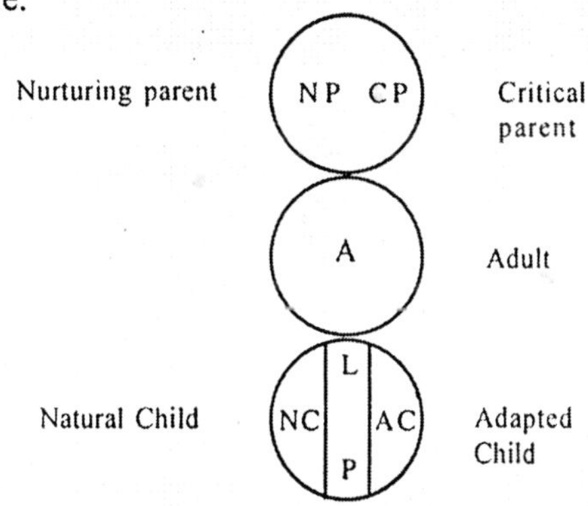


LP= Little Professor
Functional Diagram

Little professor is the intuitive and creative part of the child ego-state.

The adapted child may be manifested as compliant child, rebellious child or manipulative child.

The important point in our context is how one ego-state matches or conflicts with another ego-state in interpersonal relations. James and Jongeward noted that anything that happens between people will involve a transaction between their ego-states. When a message is given out by one person it is done with the expectation of a response. All such interpersonal transactions can be classified as *complementary, crossed* and *ulterior*.

Transactions are complementary if the message sent, or the behaviour exhibited by one person's ego-state receives the expected response from the other person's ego-state.

When the message sent by one person's ego-state is reacted to by an incompatible and unexpected ego-state of the other person the transaction is said to be crossed.

Ulterior transactions are damaging for interpersonal relations. These occur when two ego-states of a single person are involved. His words may indicate one ego-state while they may have been uttered from another.

While using PRD in villages the PRD team should be conversant with the theory of ego-states, the clues indicating various states and about the nature of interpersonal transactions. This will help the team in communicating and rapport building with the villagers. Initially the villagers may be unwilling to communicate and they will possibly be in the parent or child ego-state. The task of the team would be to intelligently guide the conversation (using their knowledge of TA) so that villagers can be brought to the adult ego-state. This is necessary because it is believed that communication, problem identification and solving, which are important constituents of the PRD exercise are done best when everybody has reached the adult ego-state.

One striking feature that the visiting team will notice when they reach the village is that villagers like any ordinary human being want recognition. The rapport building with villagers can be made easier if they are given recognition by the team members. This can be done by the use of strokes. Strokes are a way of giving recognition to individuals. The diagram (that follows) is self-explanatory.

Both unconditional and conditional strokes may be positive (+) or negative (–).

Negative strokes are better than no strokes because it at least acknowledges the presence of an individual. The use of positive strokes can serve a very useful purpose by helping in rapport building with villagers and easing the way for open unhindered communication.

On the whole the tools of TA and the use of strokes will create enabling environment for easy communication with the villagers and help in changing their wrong or negative beliefs based on tradition, prejudices, etc. to new and positive beliefs that are solidly based on facts. Thus TA in combination with strokes will enable the smooth conduction of the PRA exercise which forms one of the most important components of PRD.

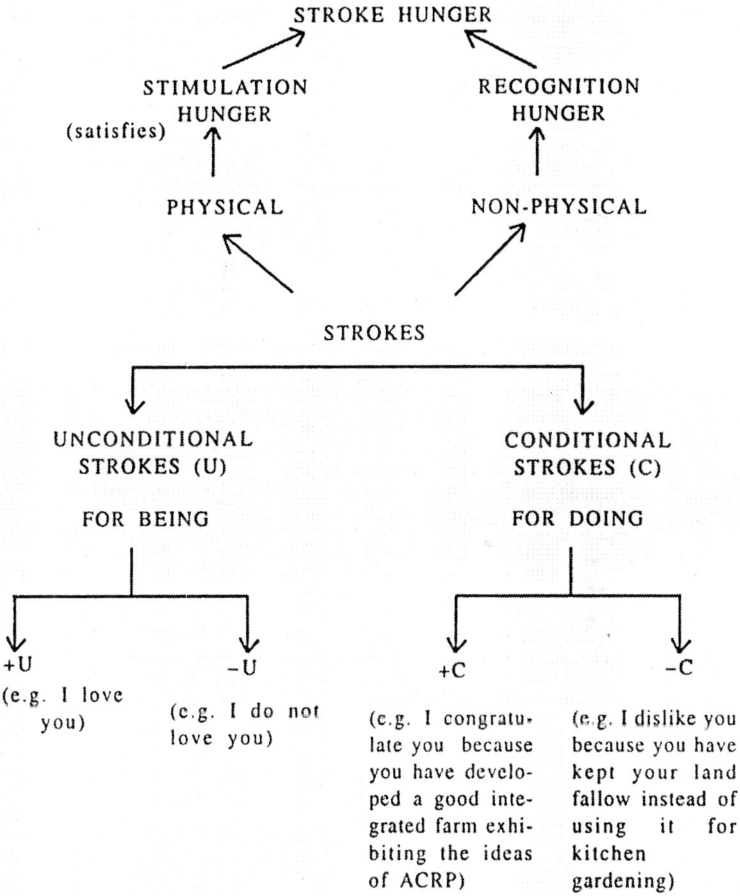


*Note* : +C and –C imply positive and negative conditional strokes respectively and +U and –U for positive and negative unconditional strokes respectively.

## ACTION LEARNING

Another important tool of Participatory Rural Development (PRD) is Action Learning, an idea introduced and developed by Reg Revans. Action learning in combination with Participatory Rural Appraisal (PRA) and Transactional Analysis (TA) constitutes the whole gamut of techniques that we call PRD. Though primarily a management tool, action learning can be and has been successfully used for achieving development objectives.

Action Learning revolves around the philosophy that men begin to learn from each other and with each other, only when they understand they do not know the answer to some problems but are jointly obliged to find them. It is an exploration of our ignorance and the consequent search for new questions that may be helpful in finding ways out of it. The steps of the Action Learning process can be loosely identified as follows. The problems should be identified by further investigating into the symptoms, then there should be a brainstorming session for sorting out problems and their solutions, next the outcome of proposals should be reported to the PRD team for evaluation and review of progress and prospects. In other words, Action Learning can be defined as a process based on taking on more crucial development related problems and, in real time, analysing their dynamics, implementing proposed solutions derived from the constructive criticisms of colleagues, monitoring results and by being held responsible for these actions, learning from these results, so that future problem solving and opportunity taking is improved.

The process of Action Learning tries to achieve a much desired blend of logic and emotionality in the process of reforming and better understanding communities by giving rigour and pace to the cycle of learning and in this task it banks on the positive power of small groups. As it gives responsibility to those who suffer from the problems a sense of belongingness is developed among them and they are committed to proposed solutions. The Action Learning process creates an enabling atmosphere for generating motivation and offers the participants (PRD team) opportunities for consciously developing their own learning. It also brings out the benefits of autonomous group activity.

A feature of a sustainable society is that it can learn faster (or at the same speed) than the rate of change in its environment. The only resource (unit) that is capable of learning is the people who comprise a society or organisation. This simple yet important idea is symbolised by the following formula.

Rate of Learning $\geq$ Rate of change = Survival

Having had a general idea of Action Learning we can now go into the details, impeding factors, dynamics, etc. of the process.

The four key elements of the Action Learning process are:

(i) A crucial community problem;

(ii) People willing to take risk to develop themselves and their communities;

(iii) Authority to take action; and

(iv) A system for learning reflectively through reflection.

In the ABC of Action Learning Reg Revans has described four corrigible handicaps to the process of deciding honest sources of information in the conditions of uncertainty and risk. These are :

(i) The idolisation of perceived past experience;

(ii) The influence of methodologies followed in other success stories;

(iii) The effects of impulsive action;

(iv) The belittlement of subordinates.

A useful diagram that somewhat summarises the ideas regarding Action Learning discussed before is reproduced below.

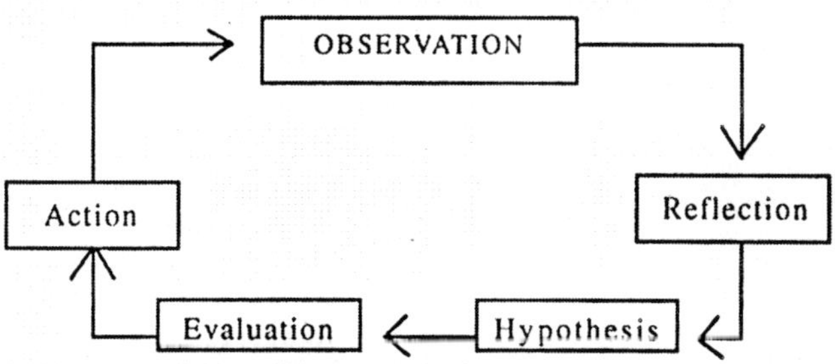


The Action Learning Cycle

Now suppose we call the development stake-holders (grassroots level people) the *clients*, and the PRD or Action Learning team the *participants*. We incorporate another entity, namely the *set adviser* who is external to the set of participants and clients but who helps in the development process. The set adviser could be the government in its role of a legislative body facilitating development (e.g., government has boosted the process of micro-planning by amending the Constitution—73rd & 74th Amendment). A *project set* is the group of development stake-holders who as group (set) help themselves and each other through the Action Learning process. The diagram below which further elucidates the Action Learning process is self-explanatory.

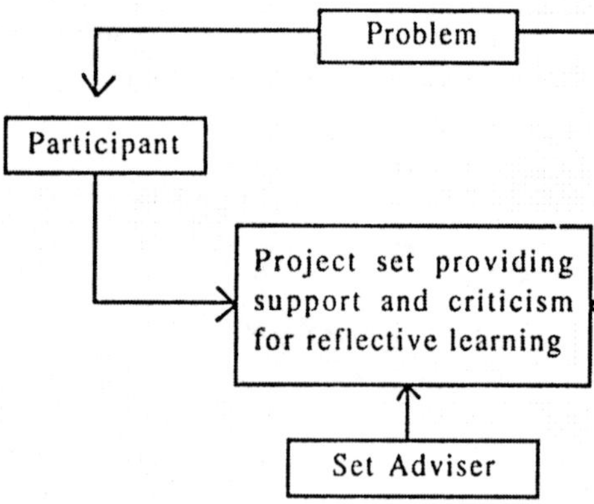


Learning (L) in general is a combination of selected past knowledge reorganised on the basis of a few discriminating questions. We call what we already know, contained in books, and from universities, polytechniques etc. programmed knowledge (P). So 'P' is the set of answers to yesterday's problems. Again 'Q' is the discriminating question put in conditions of chaos and uncertainty where no definite answer exists. 'Q' may lead us to a course of action rather than an answer. Then we can use the symbols to write the following formula:

$$L = P + Q$$

Schools, universities, etc. go about teaching *'P'* while Action

Learning tries to produce, capture or discover *'Q'*. The process of Action Learning makes it clear to the participants that no one but the problem owner can solve his/her problem although others can be very helpful. Again through the Action Learning exercise one will find that the political system which essentially resists change, has to be manipulated if a change is to take place as a result of action taken. So Action Learning becomes easier when there is positive political will.

The stages (phases) through which the development stake-holders and the PRD team have to pass when they use the Action Learning method to achieve development goals can be abstracted as follows:

| *Phase* | *Naming* | *Questions* |
|---|---|---|
| (1) Forming | 'Getting started' | 'Who are you?' 'Why are we here?' 'What is the work we can do together?' |
| (2) Action | 'Workshop' | 'How can I realise my project or vision?' 'How can I overcome my blocks?' 'Where can I get specific help and information on....?' |
| (3) Reflection | 'What is self-help?' | 'Why am I doing what I'm doing?' 'What is help & is it helpful?' Who am I and what is my role?' |

An important role in the Action Learning programme is played by the *initiator*. The initiator needs to play the role of adviser as well as that of programme manager. In the context of participatory planning and development the initiators are the government represented by its officials and the panchayat functionaries. The expectations and desires which are to emerge as answers to the questions in each of the three circles (see diagram below) are not easy to reconcile. This job of reconciliation which depends on successful selling and advisory work naturally is the responsibility of the adviser.

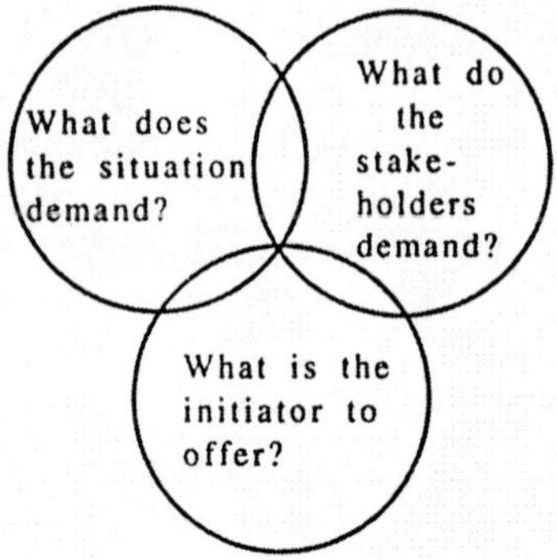


The following list of DOs and DON'Ts may be useful to anyone running an Action Learning Programme.

*DOs :*

(1) As you are introducing a change in activity be careful to treat it properly.

(2) Prepare fully.

(3) Talk to everyone about it.

(4) Be very concerned about clients (development stake-holders).

(5) Get participants (PRD team) to prepare to face what they will go through.

(6) Protect the programme at initial stages.

(7) Do a cost/benefit analysis.

(8) Try to keep the budget reasonable.

(9) Let the participants (PRD team) manage as much as possible.

(10) Be a set adviser and /or a participant.

(11) Get first class, trustworthy, supportive and creative people to work with you on the programme.

(12) Record what is happening.

(13) Consider the programme as a product.

(14) Use your own initiative, judgement and creativity.

*DON'Ts*

(1) Don't be overconfident. You will not be able to control all the outcomes.

(2) As problems are continuously changing in shape and dimension do not be disheartened or surprised if people say the problem has not been solved.

(3) Do not blindly imitate previous or present examples.

(4) Don't take the above DOs and DON'Ts as binding.

The following section summarises what has been described earlier and tries to convey a clear systematic picture of various aspects of Action Learning. Action learning is of use if:

(1) the solution to a problem is not known by anyone,

(2) nobody knows the way out of the complex situation (though there would be different opinions about the best way),

(3) there aren't enough people who can pose the right questions in situations of uncertainty, and

(4) very few people can be found, who can take risks in trying situations and produce good results.

How to begin Action Learning

(1) The participants (PRD team) will need real problems/ opportunities to work.

(2) The mindset of important people would have to be changed so that the programme would bring a change in the way things are done.

(3) People like owners of the problems (development stakeholders), individuals/groups who are significant in the problem and departments which have bearing on the problem will have to be involved.

(4) Line management will need to be involved in deciding the forms of the programme.

Keeping in mind the various guidelines while not totally ignoring flexibility the PRD team can achieve a lot by using Action Learning techniques in combination with the other tools mentioned earlier.

## Conclusion

If the project team visiting the village goes about doing PRA without properly defreezing the people then the exercise will be futile. Even if the villagers imbibe some ideas for the time being they will forget these as soon as the PRA team leaves. This is because the villagers were not sensitised properly. This is where Transactional Analysis and the use of strokes come in. The use of strokes by the PRD team will increase the confidence of the village people and they will go about solving their problems with greater belief in oneself. Again when the team first visits the village they find that the villagers are communicating with them from a critical parent or child ego-stage. As these ego-states are not conducive to further discussions and problem solving the team members have to bring the villagers to the adult ego-state. In the adult ego-state rational discussions based on objective facts are easy and unhindered. Thus TA will help the PRD team in identifying the ego-states and using techniques to convert other ego-states to adult, so that PRA exercise that follows is facilitated. Throughout the PRA exercise the knowledge of TA will facilitate smooth intercourse among the team members and the villagers. Communication in adult ego-state will ensure achievement of best obtainable benefits from the exercise assuming that Action Learning is incorporated. There will be little use of doing PRA if the experience of the villagers are not used in further enriching the collective knowledge that is used for suggesting solutions. This is what Action Learning teaches us. Unless the PRA team and the villagers sit together and analyse feedback that emerges, the suggested proposals of previous PRA exercise cannot be evaluated. PRA is no more a dynamic concept unless Action Learning is used to supplement it. Action Learning helps in refining the proposals over time, i.e., it distillates continuous improvement of the participatory planning process. The group approach that is an essential part of PRA and more specifically the brainstorming sessions of Action Learning groups also help in generating workable solutions to complex problems.

Having discussed the various tools that constitute Participatory Rural Development (PRD) we can very well understand the importance of their synthesis. The participatory planning process is such that it warrants the application of all these techniques but not in isolation. The detailed description of the various tools Participatory Rural Appraisal (PRA), Transactional Analysis (TA) and Action Learning (AL) and the methodology of using them must have already provided an idea as to why in our context they cannot be useful when applied individually.

# 6

# SUSTAINABLE DEVELOPMENT AND DECENTRALISED PLANNING

Sustainable development contains two important terms within itself, 'development' and 'sustainability'. The term development does not mean merely economic growth. It is growth in addition to change. The term gets a new dimension when attached to the concept of sustainability. The western perception of development is based on reductionist science. Science is reductionist in the sense that it provides measures for increase in productivity but does not take into account the side effects of the measure. The concept of economic growth is one-dimensional but when integrated with change, specially when it takes into consideration distributive justice, it gets its new dimension. Now added with the idea of sustainability the concept of development gets its third dimension.

The urge for rapid growth leads to irresponsible and continuous exploitation of natural resources beyond the threshold of resilience of the eco-system. In the global perspective due to mismanagement of natural resources about 25 per cent of the cultivable land is affected by soil degradation processes. About 20 per cent of the irrigated land has deteriorated because of hydromorphism, alkalization and salination. These have grave consequences on the entire environment in terms of development of plants. It leads to diminishing of recharging capacity of ground water and it lowers the purifying capacity of soil in terms of polluted water and increases soil erosion rate as well as frequency of river flooding.

The eco-system in its entirety is represented by the five hydrological constituents : *khiti* (soil), *aop* (water), *tej* (solar radiation), *marut* (wind), *byom* (atmosphere). The prime objective of sustainable development should be to maintain equilibrium in the hydrodynamic system. Hydrodynamic circulation leading to sustainable eco-system is represented by balanced open system based on the interdependency between basic natural resources like soil, water and vegetation on the one hand and geo-bio-cultural interaction on the other. When this equilibrium is lost it accelerates various dormant and active geomorphic processes on the landscape, thereby causing imbalance in the natural eco-system or hydro-dynamic circulation. Thus, this development without proper attention to sustainability has had grave consequences for the environment like desertification, loss of biodiversity, depletion of rain forest, green house effect, etc. Growing consumerism and profit maximisation motives at the behest of market economy are responsible for the plundering of natural resources leading to an economic development of dehumanising proportions. The concept of sustainable development in the real sense would be characterised by economic growth based on concern for the future, ecological principles and distributive justice. Thus sustainable development means efficient and rational utilisation of the land-water resources to meet the present as well as the future needs of the human subsystem in an eco-friendly manner. Sustainable development is becoming an increasingly popular idea on account of its inherent holistic approach. The World Commission on Environment and Development states that sustainable development ensures the needs of the present without compromising the ability of the future generations to meet their own needs. Pearce a noted economist holds that sustainable development requires policies which enable future generations to have as much wealth (or stock of wealth) as the present generation receives. The policy is that the present generation should not be profligate and incur debts that they cannot repay. Such debts could be in the form of social debts (disregard for human development), environmental debts (lack of ecological concern leading to pollution and depletion of natural resources), financial debts (borrowing beyond means) and demographic, debts (ongoing population explosion and rampant urbanisation). Mahbub-ul-Haq has discussed these issues in detail. He is of the view that every generation should have a balanced budget in the above four areas of concern. Rees (1989) discussed the difference between traditional and sustainable development. He argues that the latter 'explicitly recognizes an obligate dependence on healthy bio-sphere'. Sustainable development requires that ecological diversity and productivity in developing regions are maintained.

Daly differentiated between sustainable growth and sustainable development and found incompatibility of continuing economic growth while achieving sustainability. Some of the differences in these positions can be explained by the geographic focus of the authors, those who focus on the north tend to stress on the limits to growth and those who look to the south tend to stress on the need for growth.

Redclift maintains that "sustainable development means more than seeking a compromise between the natural environment and the pursuit of economic growth. It means a definition of economic development which recognises the limits of sustainability; having structural as well as natural origins." In particular he notes the importance of the neo-Malthusian perspective. Malthus (1878) concluded that a population cannot exceed its resources without famine or disease, providing a natural check on population growth.

In reference to agriculture, Conway and Barbier define sustainability as "the ability to maintain productivity whether of field, firm or nation in the face of stress or shock." Stress may be of various types like increasing salinity, erosion, or debt. Thus sustainability is nothing but the continuation of productivity withstanding all types of stress. They argue that sustainability is only one of the four aspects of agricultural development, the others being productivity (the absolute amount produced), stability (i.e., how reliable is production) and equitability (i.e., whether all received an equal share of production). Sustainability, in this context, becomes a possible objective to be set off against other goals of development. The three aspects of agricultural development, i.e., productivity, stability and equitability, along with our goal of sustainability, are mutually exclusive. There are many instances. Large irrigation projects may increase productivity but at the expense of sustainability and equitability. Use of pesticides and chemical fertilizers for increasing productivity may in the long run cause different diseases increasing human misery and hence cannot be sustainable. Therefore, efficiency in production alone cannot be the criterion to determine the desirability of sustainable growth. Again the question regarding trade-off between sustainability and economic efficiency can be raised. Economic efficiency can be interpreted in two ways—private efficiency and social efficiency. Private efficiency deals with efficiency from the standpoint of private profit whereas social efficiency deals with optimum allocation of resources from the standpoint of society as a whole in the Pareteian sense. Pareto optimality states a situation where further reallocation is impossible without harming at least one individual. This introduces an element of equity into the definition of efficiency. Private efficiency as it deals with private benefit (i.e., profit it may reap at the cost of social benefit) may go against sustainability in the long run. Again it may so happen that socially optimal solutions may contradict sustainability of production. As for example, Green Revolution may maximise production for the society as a whole but it may not be eco-friendly, hence environmentally not sustainable. Environment pollution in our country has been caused by the intensive use of chemicals as a part of intensive cultivation techniques. The ecological degradation in rural India can also be ascribed to the extension of HYV seed cultivation on the marginal and submarginal dry land (as such land need more chemical fertilizers) and deforestation. There may be trade off between private and social efficiency and between both of these and sustainability. The Green Revolution, an important indicator of India's economic growth, has witnessed the persistence of poverty in the midst of increasing prosperity of the landed farmers. The immiserisation hypothesis (i.e., growing income disparity among the different categories of farmers in different areas of the country) of Green Revolution is closely linked to the polarisation and proletarisation hypothesis and consequential adverse effect on wages. Thus in order to achieve economic growth, as expressed by increased agricultural production, India has to forgo her goal of equity, justice and poverty eradication, i.e., sustainable development.

Pezzey makes three points about sustainability criteria: they are long-term, they derive from a desire for intra-generational and inter-generational justice.

Thus the concept of sustainability as discussed by Pezzey refers to an all-encompassing ecological sustainability. The world conservation strategy also argues that development and conservation are not incompatible. Citing the cases where poverty had led to environmental degradation in support of this argument, the report stressed that growth is not only possible with protection of environment, it is essential to it. It is possible to have per capita output growing without limits, although this result is dependent on high technical progress and resource conservation policies. Sustainable development is a process of social and economic betterment that satisfies the needs and values of all interest groups without foreclosing future options. Sustainability thus demands the creation of a political order in which control of natural resources rests, to the maximum extent possible, with local communities who are dependent on those resources; and decision making within the community is as participatory, open and democratic as possible. The more this happens the more we will move towards sustainable development.

Redclift argues that it is not sufficient to consider sustainable development with a local focus. He believes that it is essential to use a concept of sustainable development which recognises the international structures. These may be responsible for determining whether or not sustainable livelihoods realizable for the poor are compelled to destroy resources necessary to free them from starvation and poverty. Even the actions of the rich have resulted in environmental damage or degradation. This point has also been discussed by Mahbub-ul-Haq who argues that there are important distinctions between developed and developing countries in the matter of environmental concerns. The concept of sustainable development varies from nation to nation. While the rich nations may be much concerned with problems such as global warming, dispersal of hazardous wastes, etc., the poor nations may have to survive for the time being by destroying natural resources and thus discounting the future at a higher rate than the rich. The poor cannot and need not adopt the environmental standards of the rich. The 'silent' emergencies of diseases (trachoma, schistosomiasis, etc.) are far more important to the poor nations than the highly publicised environmental emergencies of ozone layer depletion, global warming, etc.

From the above discussion it appears that sustainability implies fairness to the future. It means that all forms of total stock of wealth must not be depleted. It is consistent with the view that environmental wealth is not depleted as long as that depletion is compensated for by building up other forms of wealth, e.g., human and capital wealth. If man-made wealth is run down the environmental capital must be built up to compensate.

The decision to use the correct value of capital depends on finding the right prices. The price mechanism for man-made capital works well but pricing the environment is more difficult because the environment is surely beyond price. But anyway, there are also few markets in environmental services. Though we do not buy and sell the services of the ozone layer, to say that environment is beyond price is highly restrictive. If it means that an environment is infinitely valuable then the logical outcome is that we should not do anything to harm any form of environmental capital. But this, as a rule, would stultify human existence.

Even though environmental services are rarely sold in the market it is possible to get some idea of what these values would be if only there was a market for it. This is the economists' idea of a *shadow price,* the price that would rule if environmental goods and services were traded in right amount. Shadow price exists for all commodities whether they are marketed or not. Shadow prices are the prices that would rule if resources in the economy were optimally allocated. But we cannot leave the environmental capital to unfettered market forces to secure the right amount of environmental capital. Market economics tends to behave as if environmental services are free goods, gifts of nature. Economics and environment interact in a pervasive way. But it is an inescapable fact that economics cannot function without materials and energy and both will reappear in natural environment as wastes.

The growing world population, the demand for foodgrains and the demand for other types of food, fuel and fibre puts immense pressure on agricultural land, stocks of water, fish and timber. An estimated 60 per cent of the deforestation in developing countries is a result of expanding agriculture.

Natural resources will have to be managed with great care. Failure to accept the fact that natural resources are ultimately in finite supply, and failure to understand the divergence between private and social costs of resource exploitation are root causes of many environmental problems like erosion of deforested hill slopes, release of carbon dioxide by land clearing fires and loss of biological diversity as a result of poorly controlled logging.

The above discussion makes it clear that though environment is very important to us where sustainable development is concerned, the preservation of the same is not the only final goal. It is just a means to an end, the end being the sustenance and development of human life and living conditions in this planet. This has been argued by Mahbub-ul-Haq and many others before him.

1. Participatory development is essential for at least two reasons:
   (a) It strengthens civil society and the economy by empowering groups, communities and organisations to negotiate with institutions and bureaucracies, thus influencing public policy and providing a check on the power of the government.
   (b) It enhances the efficiency, effectiveness and sustainability of development programmes.
2. Participatory development, or what is sometimes referred to as popular participation, may be defined as a process by which people play an active and influential role in shaping decisions that affect their lives. Popular participation may involve difficult and long processes but brings many benefits—the contribution of local knowledge, an increased chance of objectives and outputs being relevant to perceived needs, greater efficiency and honesty among officials and contractors because they are under public scrutiny, ownership of the activity by community based organisations. Through empowerment, participation can also lead to changes in knowledge, skills and the distribution of power across individuals and communities, thus improving social equality.
3. Empowerment is essential to participatory development. Empowerment is enhanced when the organisations in which people participate are democratic in approach, and committed to strengthening the capacity of people to generate and influence development at various levels, increasing their access to and influence over resources and institutions including groups hitherto marginalised, such as low-income population and particularly women.

For sustainable human development we need sustainable people's organisations which can best manage the developmental process. Poverty, which is the core problem for millions in this country, can be best dealt with if a sustainable grassroots organisation, which has full knowledge of the drawbacks, potentials, and needs of the people, is involved in poverty alleviation programmes. Poverty has often been a factor contributing to environmental degradation. Human suffering in the form of abject poverty is due to a host of factors like repetition of traditional practices, collapse of local institutions, deforestation and soil erosion in small farmers' fields. Therefore, there is a need for mutually reinforcing package of technology, committed services and strong political will. Here land reform is of paramount importance because without land reform a long term interest in strengthening the production and infrastructure of the farm will be lacking. So a sustainable network of local institutions is of utmost necessity to help effectively in implementing the developmental schemes as well as family welfare schemes. With the above facts in mind the 73rd and 74th Constitution Amendments were made. Its broad objectives were:

(a) to provide more empowerment to rural people so that they can shape their own destinies and build a sustainable society,
(b) to enhance the capability of the rural people for undertaking all types of developmental activities with effective participation, and
(c) to alter the administrative structure at the rural level through PRIs.

The PRI is not a new concept in this country. As discussed elsewhere the idea of PRI was being mooted and experimented with for a long time. Yet there were big lacunae. Though it had been understood that sustainable people's organisations were indispensable for reaching out to the people at the grassroots level for sustainable human development, there was no constitutional sanction for the same. The PRI led a fevered existence.

With the 73rd and 74th Constitution Amendments the PRI has been made mandatory for all states. Moreover, in Article 243G of the Constitution Amendment Act(s) a host of areas (basically related to agriculture) have been handed over to the panchayat. From now on the PRI, headed by its apex body the Zilla Parishad, will have full authority and independence in framing plans for the areas mentioned in the article.

So, now the PRI has constitutional sanction and being in contact with the people at the grassroots level it can be the best instrument for decentralised planning leading to sustainable development. PRI being a people's organisation can be the best planner for the people, for decentralised planning has as one of its chief objectives the upliftment of the downtrodden. An organisation where the members come from these lower rungs of society is naturally best suited for improving their lot. That people are most important to planners, and that sustainable development is and should be people-centred has been ratified by the 73rd and 74th Amendment of the Indian Constitution. Participatory development can take place when stakeholders take active part.

Stakeholder's participation is defined as the process whereby all those with an interest (stakeholder) play an active role in decision-making and in the consequent activities which affect them.

Stakeholder's participation ensures that projects are more efficient, effective and sustainable. They are more efficient because by involving all interested parties a wider spectrum of knowledge is available that supports better design and implementation; financial and other costs may also be shared. They are more effective because Stakeholders' varied interests have been identified and addressed in the design; and shared ownership of the project means there is a greater chance of achieving the intended outcome. They are more sustainable because people are encouraged to use their knowledge and take initiatives and they gain skills and confidence to maintain the benefits once the project stops.

Stakeholder's participation is wider in meaning than community or beneficiary participation. It is a concept which takes into account the interests and concerns of all people affected by the project. It can help the planners in exploring the potential of participation in a whole range of projects which do not directly involve identifiable and discrete communities, railways for example or teacher training projects. It also allows the planner to see himself as just one of the Stakeholders with his own interests and perspective—a perspective which can influence and affect the participation of the others concerned, just as they can influence the development administrator.

The degree of participation of the various stakeholders can vary at different stages in the delivery of planning for development according to their identification of activity to be funded, decision making and planning; the bearing costs, implementation, receipts of benefits, monitoring and evaluation.

From a technical viewpoint, the appropriate stages and the kind of participation should be decided upon in relation to the local social and institutional situation as well as to the management requirements for the nature of the assistance being provided. But decisions about the extent and type of participation are not only technical but also political.

Stakeholders have varying degrees of power to influence outcomes and also to decide which other Stakeholders may be invited to participate and to what extent. From any stakeholder's perspective, participation can be seen as a spectrum model with a range of possiblities from being informed through consultation, partnership, delegation and ultimately to being in control. Those with less power want greater participation in management of resources and access to benefits, while those with more power are usually reluctant to give it up.

Enhancing participation by all stakeholders may, therefore, reveal a conflict of interests. For any project there should be negotiation with all stakeholders. To find good enough practical outcome is a situation of possible paradox, one where we want to take decisions based on our own values while seeking to integrate into the decision-making process the potentially different values of other stakeholders. Where poor women and men are invloved priority must go to ensure that their participation brings benefits rather than greater disadvantages. If the negotiations are seen as a zero-sum game then the less powerful will usually lose. Projects need to be implemented so that the poor are better off, whilst ensuring that the rich do not perceive themselves as losers.

Participation is an objective as well as a means for any human development related social activity. This is true also of projects with economic or sectoral goals. In all cases the project framework should make this clear.

Decentralised planning, with its goal of sustainable human development, has been facilitated greatly by the amendment of the Constitution. Sustainable human development entails people's participation and the necessity of people's organisations which the

Constitution Amendment has provided for by making the PRI mandatory. The DPC is a unit under the Zilla Parishad (district level Panchayat body) comprising both administrative and Panchayat officials. So it will now be possible to have various sub-plans for the same district depending on the diversities existing in it. Similar, will be the case for blocks and even villages. The 73rd and 74th Constitution Amendments will help greatly in promoting the idea and practice of people-centred participatory planning which is an inalienable part of a successful decentralised planning exercise. For decentralisation, as we know by now, is primarily for the upliftment of the people from the grassroots level. Otherwise sustainability cannot exist in its most desired sense. This is possible when planning is participatory, when needs of people from the lowest rungs of society are appraised and prioritised as the planner moves upwards to each higher level for the final selection of projects and allocation of funds, where planners harmoniously work together with the people for whom they plan.

# 7

# PRI AS THE LONG-TERM SUSTAINABILITY SOLUTION

Decentralised planning means planning at different levels, that is, multi-level planning. This concept of decentralised planning is not new but has gained currency in view of India's experience of rural development. From the very beginning, apart from infrastructural development with basic heavy and core industries, planners have never lost sight of rural development. Community development started in 1960s with the avowed goal of developing rural areas. Block development officers were at the helm of block administration. They were expected to bring about the metamorphosis of a stagnant rural society plagued by illiteracy, very poor sanitation and host of other socio-economic ills. The concept of community development on a theoretical plane is nice but due to inherent weaknesses in community development programmes it did not materialise. During 1970s, the government came forward with certain poverty alleviation programmes to make a frontal attack on poverty. The people on whom these programmes have been imposed have no sense of belongingness. The old situation prevails. The government officials become the donors and the people concerned become the recipients. This relation of *mai baap* persists. People, instead of occupying the centre-stage of development, have become the object of development.

Primacy of people or people's participation, which is the cornerstone of any sustainable programme, is lost. The present bureaucracy, instead of being instrument of change, is only administering different anti-poverty programmes. Therefore, in the process these so-called target-oriented anti-poverty schemes become more important than the content. The end, that is rural development, is lost sight of and the means, that is mere administration of the schemes, get pre-eminence. Here bureaucracy, representing the government, owns the schemes. They are not serving as facilitators. Therefore, people do not shoulder any responsibility to ensure the success of the scheme. Entire planning process is deficient as it is only done at the top level. The administrators have only superficial knowledge of the local conditions. At times they do not possess any knowledge at all. The officials are instructed to fulfil the targets. Thus the programme becomes highly bureaucratic. Considering the complexities of social structure in Indian villages more dynamic and flexible concept of community development suited to local needs is required. The community development programmes failed to take into account the ground realities existing in Indian villages.

Organisationally the creation of blocks as units of development was good. It was expected that the isolation of villages with all its limitations will no longer be there. As in the words of Nehru, "People were to be invested with a sense of intimate partnership." The sense of intimate partnership can arise only out of active participation of all stakeholders. But the fundamental problem lies here. As some money was flowing in the hitherto stagnant village society in the name of developmental work nexus was immediately created between new found bureaucracy and rural elite, i.e., the landed aristocracy, to siphon off the money. Thus community development programmes, instead of reducing rural inequality, further aggravated it. Developmental programmes had marginal impact over the village masses. The village community participated unequally. People regarded these programmes as government schemes for rural upliftment and expected the government to serve as a parent figure for doing everything on their behalf. This continued dependence on the government was against the ethos of the community development programme, thus upsetting the philosophy of self-help. Therefore it is amply clear that this bureaucracy-led-development cannot bring any appreciable change in the static rural society inhibited by abject poverty, malnutrition and a rigid mentality. The genesis of the failure of community development programme has been succinctly summarised by the survey report prepared by National Institute of Community Development, Hyderabad; the report was as follows : The first and foremost task in achieving community development is an increase in agricultural production; the next goal is social welfare where the main concern of panchayats include a wide range of amenities, schools, roads, street lights, health, sanitation and drinking water. Very few people thought that improving the conditions of the weaker section was the goal of the programme. They conclude that village people have their own way of recognising the usefulness of the programmes which are by and large conceived in New Delhi. The villagers accepted their usefulness only in terms of specific benefits and not in terms of philosophies like group efforts and rural democracy. Integrated rural development which community development looked forward to was a failure due to its inherent top-down approach. Involvement of people in planning cannot come without empowerment. Development and empowerment are two distinct phases of progress. Due to good implementation of any rural development scheme there might be some alleviation of poverty but that progress will not be sustainable unless the people concerned are properly empowered to take their own decisions. Unless they are given any decision-making power, people's involvement will be a distant dream. When properly empowered they become accountable to themselves. This accountability is different from bureaucratic accountability. Bureaucrats are accountable to their superiors and they are supposed to stay for a brief period. Due to their frequent transfers the bureaucrats usually do not develop any attachment to their work. They work as per routine without any commitment to the programme. But for successful implementation of any rural development programme, bureaucratic commitment is indispensable. In our country with so much poverty, illiteracy and other social rigidities positive state intervention through bureaucracy committed to rural development will create an environment conducive to empowerment.

Panchayats, though functioning for a long time, got their constitutional status after 73rd Amendment. After all these years of functioning, specially in West Bengal where we had four successful elections of Panchayats, our success stories are few in number. People's involvement in the decision-making process is a fundamental criterion. But how will the illiterate or ignorant person take part in decision making? Panchayats are supposed to create an environment suitable for educating the rural masses. But Panchayats are yet to take an initiative in this regard. Just to share power with people at the grassroots level demands more and more decentralisation of power.

Devolution, which is the strongest form of decentralisation of power, has been given to the Panchayats after the 73rd Amendment of the Constitution. And Panchayats have been asked to carry further devolution of power through *Gram Samsad* and *Gram Sabha.* The idea that decentralisation should stop with him and it should not percolate below is quite characteristic of an average human psyche. Due to this psyche there is an apprehension that panchayats may ultimately turn out to be another rigid organisation where the prime object of people's participation will be lost. Despite these panchayats are the ultimate hope. It has been experienced that with development democracy in terms of people's participation will automatically come. But it has been found to be a myth. What we need is an inversion of the order, i.e, democracy should precede development to make development more sustainable. Organisationally, panchayats in the present form are not strong enough to take care of rural development with all its technicalities. Herein comes the role of a committed bureaucracy with a positive outlook for development. At the grassroots level the block development officers and other extension officers, viz., the entire bureaucracy reflects bureaucratic will. If it is committed and development-oriented and if it is subsumed by genuine political will as reflected by Panchayats, it can really bring radical transformation to our rural society still inhibited by illiteracy, poverty and absence of basic amenities of a decent living.

Empowerment is the process of transcending a state of powerlessness. The basic difference between empowerment and development is that while the former is a fundamental issue in organising panchayat as a strategy for sustainable development, the latter gives a feeling of condescension and is not sustainable as such.

So it is clear that a decentralised planning framework which entails devolution of powers and functions from the centre downwards cannot function without people's organisations. Decentralised planning is planning for the people in a way that reflects the needs, aspirations and potentialities of a region and is based on the resources of the people. Planners working at the Centre cannot correctly know the situation prevalent at the grassroots level throughout the country. So for planning to be successful, it is absolutely necessary to hand over this task to the lowest possible level of administration and planning. The basic aim of the plan is to improve the condition of the lowest tiers of society. However, the planners or administrators are not exactly the people who are targeted by the plan. They cannot know the needs and aspirations of the poorest and deprived classes. Moreover, administrators have negative stereotypes in their minds about the grass-roots people and look upon them as unmotivated, lacking in leadership and looking upon the government only as the giver (themselves being passive receivers). Similarly, the development stakeholders or people from the grassroots level have negative stereotypes regarding bureaucrats, that they are unaccountable, corrupt, high handed, unmotivated as they are easily transferable. To remove these difficulties what is needed is sustainable people's organisations, which work side by side and in harmony with the administrators, planners and line department officials in preparing the plan. One important question that naturally comes up is regarding the correct mix of technical expertise and people's participation in the planning exercise. Undoubtedly, it is a two-way process. The team of planners should consult not only the elected panchayat body members about their felt needs, aspirations and more importantly regarding resources and their potentials, constraints, technical matters like superiority of a breed of cattle, lessons from the past and present schemes and policies, etc. The goals of decentralised planning will be furthered if in the course of discussions the planning teams explain to the villagers the problem of choice (i.e., planning) between alternative uses of scarce resources and also the policy decision to tilt the balance in favour of the deprived sections. In a way it will strengthen decentralised planning and as such dialogue will minimise the adverse effects of a plan which cannot take care of all needs and aspirations of the deprived. The dialogue should go on continuously from plan formulation to all the stages of implementation. People's organisations are comprised of the very people for whom planning is undertaken. People are after all the end for whom planning is undertaken. So the primary focus of the planners should be the maximum possible external manifestation of the inherent human potentialities. To ensure this, people have to be placed at the centre of all planning activities. If bettering the lives of the deprived is the end then we cannot work without bringing them to the fore. We need sustainable people's organisations which being close to the people can best know their needs and potentials while at the same time help in developing a sense of belongingness among them failing which they will always be alienated from the schemes and projects of the government or funds that the government spends for them. Such alienation is dangerous as it does not foster development of human capabilities. Rather it stultifies motivation. Lack of motivation has a negative pull, and leads in failure to move forward unless pushed by the government.

A people's organisation can play a big role in generating a sense of belongingness. It will make people care for the works that the government undertakes and look upon them as their own. Corruption in expenditure of government money during execution of various projects and schemes can be better dealt with. This is because the people, who have developed a sense of belongingness, will help in monitoring the activities taken up by the government. There may be people's audit of accounts and a demand for greater transparency from and accountability of government officials. However, these will come to be only if a stable people's organisation has managed to develop a strong sense of belongingness among grassroots level people. Once the people are motivated they can take care of many of their problems with little or no government assistance. So there will surely be movements in the direction of decentralisation and self-sufficiency.

It is clear that a sustainable people's oganisation is a *sine qua non* for a successful decentralised planning system. Now people's organisations have existed in this country for a long time and the most important of these is the Panchayat. The creation of panchayats has been commented upon in the Directive Principles of State Policy of the Indian Constitution. However, as the Directive Principles are not justiciable the panchayat bodies had a miserable existence in many states of our country. In many cases elections to these people's bodies were not held for long or the results of these elections were manipulated. Decisions taken by panchayats were also ignored in many cases. Politicians interfered with the working of these people's organisations time and again. They also enjoyed few liberties as far as fund appropriation, expenditure and planning were concerned.

With the 73rd Amendment of the Indian Constitution this scene is about to change. This important amendment has given panchayats the much needed constitutional sanction, thus freeing it from the shackles of bad politics. In its various articles the 73rd Amendment has made the holding of Panchayat elections mandatory within a stipulated time, given powers of expenditure and fund appropriation to Panchayats and power of preparing plans for economic development and social justice (in agriculture and related fields). This amendment also describes the panchayat as a self-government institution which will have three tiers of governance—*Gram Panchayat, Panchayat Samiti* and *Zilla Parishad.*

As the Panchayat or the PRI is a people's organisation and as its sustainability has been guaranteed by the 73rd Amendment we can expect that it will go a long way in fulfilling the goals of decentralisation. Again the 11th Schedule has given the PRI the right to plan in 29 important areas and it can be reasonably hoped that people's needs and aspirations will be reflected in the planning for these areas. Not only has the 73rd Amendment given constitutional sanction to people's organisations but it has also, to a great extent, relieved the panchayat bodies from political interference.

The 73rd Amendment also instructs the governor of a state to constitute a State Finance Commission (SFC) to review the financial position of the panchayats. The SFC has to make recommendations to the governor regarding the principles which should govern distribution of the net proceeds from taxes, duties, tolls, etc. between the State and the Panchayat as well as the allocation of the same among various levels of the Panchayat. The SFC will also make recommendations to the governor regarding the principles which should govern the grants-in-aid to panchayats from the consolidated fund of the state, measures needed to improve the financial position of the panchayats and many other important financial matters. Thus constitution of the SFC has increased the power of the Panchayat bodies *vis-a-vis* the state. Panchayats now not only have the constitutional sanction but also some control over funds so that they may effectively perform the duties and execute the powers which the 73rd Amendment has vested in them. By investing the panchayats with the powers of fund appropriation and spending, this amendment has furthered the cause of decentralisation of funds.

The 74th Amendment Act along with the 12th Schedule has also helped to a great extent in decentralised planning conducted by urban bodies.

# 8

# BLOCK PLANNING METHODOLOGY

In the late 1960s the district level was identified as the appropriate level from which bottom-up planning should start. However, about a decade later it was felt that the district was not very well suited to serve the ends of decentralised planning. Thus the idea of block-level planning emerged. The Dantwala Committee Report (1978) suggested ways and means of experimenting with block-level planning. Block planning is, however, still in its infancy in India.

The broad goals of block-level planning are somewhat similar to those of decentralised planning mentioned elsewhere in this book. The global objectives of block-level planning are:

(i) to increase the income and employment of the people living in an area through optimum utilisation of its potential for growth;

(ii) to ensure that the benefits of development are reaped more by the deprived classes, small and marginal farmers, share-croppers, agricultural labourers, rural artisans, etc.;

(iii) to fulfil the minimum needs programme. This programme covers health and medical facilities, drinking water, housing, education and supply of essential commodities through public distribution system;

(iv) to set up social and economic infrastructure for achieving the objectives mentioned above;

(v) to project the interests of the poor by reorienting the existing institutions and organisations;

(vi) to protect the poor from exploitation appropriate organisations of the poor have to be built up;

(vii) to make ownership and assets progressively more egalitarian;

(viii) duration of productive employment of the poor and underemployed in their present occupation should be increased *inter alia* through technology upgradation, importing of skills and by setting up of non-exploitative institutions of credit marketing and extension; and adoption of appropriate technologies which are generally labour-intensive;

(ix) employment of public works for alleviating residual unemployment.

The emphasis on block-level planning implies an implicit expectation, that through a search for locating development potential, strengthening of the planning machinery and better informed planning mechanism, the block-level development process would receive a boost.

This brings us to the general characteristics that a block plan should possess. These are :

(a) The language of the plan should be simple and preferably in vernacular;

(b) The means adopted by the planner to produce his proposals should be clear to the reader;

(c) The socio-economic status of the block should be taken into account during formulation of the plan; and

(d) Felt needs of the local people should be reflected in the plan.

A series of steps are followed in the preparation of the block plan:

| | | |
|---|---|---|
| *Step 1* | : | Collection of data about the area and the people. |
| *Step 2* | : | Analysis of collected data to identify problems, potentials, opportunities, needs and gaps existing in the area and among its people. |

| | | |
|---|---|---|
| *Step 3* | : | Decision regarding plan objectives. |
| *Step 4* | : | Review and modifications (if necessary) of on-going programmes to suit the pursued objectives. |
| *Step 5* | : | New project identification on the basis of clear needs. |
| *Step 6* | : | Plans for financial allocation. |

These steps are together known as *planning cycle* and are explained in detail below.

## STEP 1

In case of block planning purview, step 1 can be broadened to the wider concept of *block analysis.*

### *Block Analysis*

The block analysis will bring out the physical, economic and social situations; the disparities, the diversities and any trends that may be found in the regional economy.

From the regional economy trend the poverty and employment situations can be assessed while development potentials, problems and gaps can be later identified. Block analysis comprises six stages which follow one after the other. A brief outline of each stage is detailed now.

*Stage 1 : Decision regarding type and nature of data to be collected*

Herein the 'need-to-know' principle is used which states that data should be collected if

(a) there is a reasonable certainty that the data will be used in the analysis, and

(b) the data is needed to explain the plan to others.

The collected data will then have to be organised into a matrix or a table. Matrices can be constructed under the heads :

(a) Land and physical resources,

(b) Agriculture and allied resources,

(c) Infrastructure and services,

(d) Industry and other economic sectors, and

(e) Human resources.

A single matrix should contain data for a particular point of time. Following construction of matrices, summary tables are prepared which organises the information according to a particular theme or indicator.

*Stage 2 : Identification of disparties at Gram Panchayat (GP) level by using the block matrices and summary tables*

Gram Panchayat is the smallest (lowest) unit represented by elected members of the three-tier panchayat system and comprises one single *gram* which is the definitional notion of a village (which in turn can be defined as a collection of one or more adjacent mouzas). Disparities can be measured by comparing the data for a GP with that of the block in which the GP is situated. If it is found that a GP's performance falls below the block average then the block plan should take care to rectify it.

Some measures of disparity which can be used are :

*Numerical Disparity*

This is obtained by subtracting data of a GP from the average data of all the GPs in a block and the result is shown with the following appropriate algebraic equations:

$$\text{Percentage disparity per unit area} = \frac{\text{G P data / area of GP}}{\text{Block total/area of the block}} \times 100$$

$$\text{Percentage disparity per unit population} = \frac{\text{G P data / population of GP}}{\text{Block total/population of the block}} \times 100$$

After the disparities are calculated, a GP disparity analysis form (shown below) has to be filled up.

GP disparity analysis form

Block Name :
Number of GPs :
Area :
Population :

| | 1 Provision | 2 Provision | 3 Provision | 4 Provision |
|---|---|---|---|---|
| GP fund | | | | |
| Block Data | | | | |
| GP-wise average | | | | |
| Numerical disparity | | | | |
| Disparity per unit area | | | | |
| Disparity per unit population | | | | |

With the help of the above table the relative position of the GP *vis-a-vis* the block with respect to certain provisions can be seen clearly.

*Stage 3 : Identification of potential sectors/activities in each GP*

Potential sectors/activities are those which dominate the regional economy by generating a large part of output and employment.

A measure termed *Location Quotient* (LQ) is used to identify a potential sector/activity.

$$LQ = \frac{\text{Percentage labour engaged in a sector in the GP}}{\text{Percentage labour engaged in a sector in the block}}$$

An LQ value greater or less than one would indicate greater or less than average respectively prevalence of the sector in a GP.

After the LQ is calculated for all GPs the following form has to be filled up and with this stage 3 ends.

Potential activity/sector identification form

| LQ calculation for activities/sectors | | | |
|---|---|---|---|
| GP | Activity 1 | Activity 2 | Activity 3 |
| GP 1 | | | |
| GP 2 | | | |
| Block | | | |
| LQ GP 1 | | | |
| LQ GP 2 | | | |

*Stage 4 : Prediction of changes in variables*

Any change in variables is predicted with the help of a future trend which is based on information about previous years. Trends that should be calculated for block level are:

(a) trends in agricultural output,
(b) trends in population growth,
(c) trends in employment,
(d) trends in poverty.

At first decision has to be taken as to what variables have to be predicted. This is followed by collection of information on the variables for the previous years and finally tabulation of the collected data. After this forecasting methods are applied on the collected information.

One such simple method of forecasting is *simple extrapolation* which calculates the rate of change between two or more years (for which data is available) and projects it to the future.

*Stage 5 : Preparation of base maps*

Base maps are prepared to present information about the block in an easily comprehensible manner as opposed to texts and tables. Maps are drawn according to a definite scale. A scale shows the ratio between actual distance on the ground between two points and the distance between the same two points on the map. Base maps can be sourced from police station maps (scale 1" = mile i.e. 1:50,000) and Survey of India toposheets (scale 1" = mile i.e. 1:50,000).

However, maps of such scales are not suitable for micro-planning. For this purpose maps having a scale of about 1:10,000 would be helpful. In fact cadestral maps (scale 16" = 1 mile, i.e. 1:4,000) are most suitable for a micro planning exercise. Using such a map the hydrological, topological and other such features of an area can be studied in detail.

A base map should include information like block boundary, GP boundary and village boundary with appropriate legend, latitude, longitude, direction and contour lines, road network (various types of roads of varying importance), rivers/streams and major water bodies, administrative nodal points, important facilities and infrastructure like PHC, SHC, block vet, health unit, banks, markets, schools, major P.O., cooperatives, etc.

Two types of maps can be prepared from the base maps:

(1) General purpose or reference maps (e.g. one showing just the administrative boundaries).

(2) Special purpose or thematic maps (on a particular theme like a map showing schools, health units, banks, etc.).

*Stage 6 : Preparation of a Block Profile*

A concise block profile is prepared by using inputs from the previous stages. A block profile should consist of

(a) introduction to the block, location in the state/district, administration, basic physical features (e.g., hills, rivers, etc.),

(b) *natural resources* : mineral and similar resources, water resources, forest resources, fisheries,

(c) *human resources* : total population and its composition, patterns of population distribution,

(d) *land and agriculture* : land ownership and land use, main crops, livestock (if important),

(e) *industry* : major industries, small scale and cottage industries,

(f) *infrastructure* : major services (national highways, railways, etc.) power supply, market, financial institutions,

(g) *community facilities* : education, health and sanitation, recreation, etc.

This brings step 1, that is the Block Analysis part of formulating the block plan to an end. The next step includes analysis of collected data to identify problems, potentials, opportunities, needs and gaps existing in the block.

## STEP 2

Step 2 is necessary for framing the area specific or block specific objectives of the block plan. The objectives are derived by examining the opportunities and potentials, the problems, the needs and the gaps.

### *Opportunities and potentials*

Potentials of a block are its wealth of natural and human resources. Along with these there are important activities based on local resources of the people living here (measured by Location Quotient in the previous step). These activities and endowments together constitute potentials and opportunities. The difference between opportunity and potential can be understood in another way. When there are means to realise some potential then we say there exists an opportunity.

### *Problem*

Problem identification is done with the help of information obtained from block analysis. Thus problems can come out of GP disparity analysis described in the previous step.

### *Needs*

Needs are generally perceived or felt problems. People's needs are identified by using participatory rural development techniques which also generate a sense of belongingness and motivation among the development stakeholders. Also the consultation procedure can be used for assessing needs. After the 73rd Amendment of the Constitution the importance of people's organisation in the form of panchayats have increased a lot. Requests from Panchayat bodies are a major source of information from which objectives can be framed. It is necessary that block plans incorporate grassroots level needs expressed by people's organisations.

*Gaps*

Gaps emerge when the block situation is juxtaposed against some set standards.

The grassroots level needs can be identified by—

(1) Consultation procedure, and

(2) Participatory Rural Development (PRD).

Each of the above two procedures are expected to strengthen the other and facilitate smooth execution of the prioritisation exercise. There is a standard form which is used during the consultation procedure for recording requests and opinions from the *Gram Sabha* level. The format could be as follows :

| Block Name : | | | |
|---|---|---|---|
| GP Name : | | | |
| Request | Estimated cost (Rs.) | Reason for request | Resource |
| | | | |

Once the *Gram Sabha* formats are ready these are aggregated and approved (or modified) by the concerned *Panchayat Samiti.*

The PRD method is designed to elicit practical information on development issues in local communities and also to generate a sense of belongingness and motivation. As PRD method is basically geared towards discovering needs and involves consultation and free and open discussion there is ample scope of needs being informed by success stories and experience as well as suggestion from experts.

Once the problems, potentials and needs are identified these have to be prioritised. During prioritisation the administrative machinery has to work in close cooperation with the panchayat bodies. The following form is used during the prioritisation of problems, potentials and needs.

| Prioritising potentials, problems and needs | | |
|---|---|---|
| Potentials, problems and needs | Faced by number of GPs | Ranks |
| | | |

**STEP 3**

A set of objectives are then framed from the analysis of potentials, problems, needs and gaps. An example will make the process clear.

Example :

Potential : Groundwater available

This is rephrased to get the objective : Creation of dug wells for irrigation.

The final list of objectives is to be expressed in a precise manner along with the time schedule (for achieving the same) and quantitative indicators by which performance of each block can be monitored and judged.

**STEP 4**

This step entails a review of ongoing government schemes (whether they should be continued/modified in a particular place etc.) in the light of the objectives. Government investments in a block are made through various departmental schemes and programmes of the government such as JRY, EAS, DWCRA, etc.

There is ample scope of implementing the schemes in changing locations with varying intensity. Each scheme is judged in the light of the following :

(a) Consistency features, (b) GP disparity analysis, and (c) Inter-scheme linkage.

(a) *Consistency Features*

Consistency features mean consistency in terms of programme objectives, environmental impact and eco-friendliness (details in chapter on Environment), expansion capacity, *vis-a-vis,* use of unutilised capacity.

A table can be used to represent each of the above criteria wherein appropriate score or weightage can be attached to depict the programme or scheme's relevance in the progress of the Block/GP. Such scores weightage could be quantitative or qualitative.

(b) *GP Disparity analysis*

This analysis helps in judging the merits of a scheme/programme in reducing disparities among GPs.

A table can be drawn where each entry in the box depicts the number of GPs where disparity has been reduced in relation to the block average. In the table shown below scheme 3 turns out to be the best as far as reducing inter-GP disparities is concerned.

| | Scheme 1 | Scheme 2 | Scheme 3 |
|---|---|---|---|
| Problem 1 | 2 | 1 | – |
| Problem 2 | – | – | 3 |
| Problem 3 | 1 | 1 | 1 |
| Disparity reducing score | 3 | 2 | 4 |

(c) *Inter-scheme Linkage*

This criterion is useful in taking a decision regarding continuing or discontinuing a programme. A scheme or programme may be beneficial indirectly by having linkages with other schemes, i.e. directly or indirectly it may generate income and employment, and reduce poverty in spheres of activity which are connected with it through backward or forward linkages. A scheme having a backward linkage with another scheme should be using output of the other scheme as an input, A forward linkage implies that the scheme will provide inputs to another. Inter-scheme linkage can be portrayed with a table shown below where entries indicate the presence of linkage or interconnectivity.

| | Scheme 1 | Scheme 2 | Scheme 3 | Scheme 4 |
|---|---|---|---|---|
| Scheme 1 | – | – | X | X |
| Scheme 2 | X | X | – | X |
| Scheme 3 | X | – | X | – |
| Scheme 4 | – | – | X | – |
| Interconnectivity Score | 2 | 1 | 3 | 2 |

Scheme 3 is the first choice where interconnectivity is concerned as it has the highest interconnectivity score.

*Overall Relevance of the Scheme*

The overall relevance of a scheme is judged by cumulating or aggregating the constituency score, disparity reduction score and interconnectivity score to get a composite score.

The ongoing schemes or programmes will be adjusted in the light of the above exercise of prioritisation that gives an aggregate or overall relevance of each scheme.

**STEP 5**

New projects/schemes should be identified based on clearly felt needs. Some terms need to be explained at this point.

*Project :* It is a set of activities aimed at achieving a goal within a time frame, with assigned resources and in a specific area or region.

*Programme :* A programme is a combination of similar projects aimed at achieving a goal.

The following steps are necessary for choosing, designing and putting a project into action :

(a) Project identification
(b) Project formulation
(c) Project appraisal
(d) Project implementation
(e) Monitoring and evaluation.

Identification of a project is done by generating a project idea. A project idea, in its turn will be generated in the light of the objectives that emanate from step 3 in the block plan formulation exercise and according to the broad objectives contained in the plan documents.

These project ideas are, however, to be ranked and this prioritisation can be done with the following important principles as guidelines. Schemes which are likely to generate employment could be awarded highest priority. Second in importance are schemes which generate complementary and supplementary investments. Third comes schemes which bring unutilised resources into use. The next step deals with the making of a project plan.

*Project Plan*

It is a concise statement of the background to the project, what it is intended to achieve, what are the main inputs and expected outputs, what are the risks involved and what are the benefits expected.

The plan is drawn into a standard format called *Project Format* containing the following sections :

(a) Background
(b) Objectives
(c) Components (what the project contains)
(d) Finance
(e) Risks and assumptions
(f) Benefits and costs

This brings us to project feasibility analysis which has three components :

(i) Technical feasibility

(ii) Economic viability (encompassing social acceptability as well as financial viability)

(iii) Environmental acceptability

Tests of technical feasibility are done by the concerned departments. Financial viability is assessed by using financial analysis of cost-benefit type, say cash flow measures. Environmental acceptability test is done using a methodology called Environment Impact Assessment (EIA) wherein the impact of a project on the natural environment and health and well-being of human beings can be predicted.

These feasibility studies taken together decide the final selection or rejection of a project.

**STEP 6**

The final step in block planning deals with allocation of funds by sectors obeying the laws of demand and supply. The fund allocation is an interactive process based on democratic norms. Here qualitative and quantitative estimates of programmes and performances are considered side by side with some guiding principles of fund allocation.

The final block planning exercise is undertaken by the Block Planning Committee (BPC). The chairman of the BPC is the *Sabhapati* and the BDO is the member-secretary.

Another body called Block Level Coordination Committee (BLCC) for Banking assists the BPC by providing an estimate of institutional finance that may be invested for implementing various programmes under the purview of the block plan. BPC primarily makes a compromise between demand for funds in the form of submitted schemes/programmes and supply of funds from various sources.

Total demand can be broken up into three components :

(1) Demand from GPs

(2) Demand for block schemes

(3) Demand for departmental schemes

The largest share of the block plan fund goes towards implementation of schemes at the GP level. The demand from GPs is usually sent in the form of a group of schemes with fund estimations done on a normative basis. The block machinery implements the block schemes and a portion of the funds is allocated for this purpose. Though blocks have some responsibility in the implementation of departmental schemes rarely is there any claim on block funds, for these are included under district schemes.

Fund supply for block planning comes from four sources. The assigned fund (tied and untied) is available from district sources under recommended allocation by DPC. Institutional funds flow through BLCC while the remaining through a part of district allocations. BLCC is the block-level nodal agency for institutional funds. In this task it is guided by DLCC (District Level Coordination Committee). Another source of funds is from mobilisation of internal resources or funds. This has been facilitated by the 73rd Amendment of the Constitution which has provided opportunities for the block to generate significant resources on its own.

The other sources of funds are benefit sharing, public enterprises, donations, etc.

### Allocation Mechanism

Allocation at the block level is a decision making problem based on a participatory approach. As demand for funds is greater than the supply a balance between the two has to be ensured using commonly accepted principles of allocation for assigning the funds. The principles determining allocation are :

(a) continuing programmes,

(b) reprioritisation,

(c) negotiation and arbitration,

(d) general allocation criteria like population, area, etc.,

(e) level of development,

(f) allocation over time should be increasing,

(g) potential/lead sector allocation should be increasing over time,

(h) credit-deposit ratio,

(i) forward-backward linkage of sector/scheme,

(j) performance record in scheme implementation, and

(k) financial regularity and accounting.

Allocation is finalised by the BPC based on the above principles following the steps given below. The steps are :

(1) BPC technical team does physical review of block plan.
(2) BPC technical team does financial review of block plan.
(3) Block credit review by BLCC.
(4) Block fund allocation by sectors and schemes.
(5) Disaggregated block fund allocation by GPs and sectors/ schemes.
(6) Iterative allocation exercise by considering steps 1 to 5 till deficit is within the means and conflicts are resolved.
(7) Steps 1 to 6 to be repeated till deficit is within 10 per cent of allocation so that no further review is necessitated.

The next stage is operationalising the plan which is facilitated by a transparent mechanism and building up of necessary logistics.

**PHYSICAL REVIEW**

| Sector/ Scheme | Unit | Performance | | | |
|---|---|---|---|---|---|
| | | Period t1 to Period t2 | | | |
| | | Target | Achievement | Anticipated Achievement | Tentative Target |
| 1 | | | | | only |
| 2 | | | | | assumed |
| 3 | | | | | + |
| . | | | | | |
| . | | | | | |
| . | | | | | |
| n | | | | | proposed |
| Total | | | | | |

FINANCIAL REVIEW

| Sector/ Scheme | Performance (lakhs) | | | | |
|---|---|---|---|---|---|
| | Period t1 to Period t2 | | | | |
| | Approved Outlay | Actual Expenditure | Approved Outlay | Anticipated Expenditure | Proposed Outlay |
| 1 | | | | | only |
| 2 | | | | | assumed |
| 3 | | | | | + |
| . | | | | | |
| . | | | | | |
| . | | | | | |
| n | | | | | proposed |
| Total | | | | | |

# 9

# MONITORING AND EVALUATION TECHNIQUE OF DEVELOPMENT SCHEMES

Development schemes in all cases should be followed by the twin processes of *Monitoring* and *Evaluation.* These two parallel systems act as check and balance to see that the development schemes fulfil the desired objectives in keeping with people's needs. There is a basic difference of focus between these two processes of monitoring and evaluation.

Monitoring refers to re-examination of tasks, activities and expenses incurred in course of initiating the scheme to make sure that activities abide by original layouts. Through this process we may ascertain deviations from original plans. Subsequent follow-up actions may be duly decided upon. It may also become necessary to make revisions in the original plan to make plans more consistent with ground realities. Thus monitoring is a process of ascertaining systematically and objectively, the extent of congruence between actual results and original expectations of the people as well as objectives of the programmes. Monitoring then aims to ensure the congruence between activities and plans.

Evaluation, in contrast, involves critical assessment of development objectives. It is essentially a process of debunking objectives that are taken for granted. It is a mechanism to check whether the objectives set out at the inception are still valid after completion, or whether some changes are required. It becomes necessary to assess development objectives from time to time because of several imperatives, for example (i) the underlying assumption built into the structure of the programme may be invalidated; (ii) questions relating to environmental safety may crop up displacing previous assumptions; (iii) it may become necessary to reformulate the objectives themselves to make for greater focus in the face of newly gained experience. Thus evaluation itself becomes a process of cognition for the development officials.

Another difference between monitoring and evaluation is along the temporal scale. Monitoring is conducted at frequent intervals say, monthly or quarterly while the project is being implemented. In contrast to this, evaluation is conducted at longer time gaps say, two or three years, only after some experience has been gained about the implementation and its impact. The processes of monitoring and evaluation then act in consonance as one medium of feedback and reflection.

The process of monitoring may be diagramatically represented :

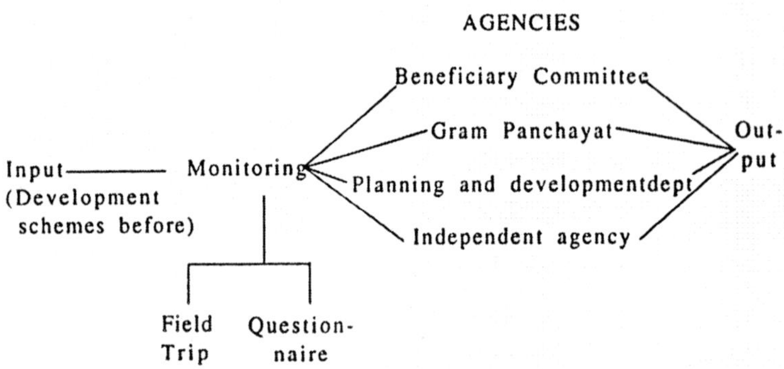


The key parameters, along which the successes and failures of the development schemes are going to be monitored, are to be evolved by members of the monitoring agency in cooperation with the initiators of the development project.

Unlike monitoring which is basically a technical procedure, evaluation is to be a critical, value laden task. It may be conducted either by an internal team or by some other external agency. Since evaluation is a task involving subjective judgements it is preferable if it is conducted by external, independent agencies. A team of persons involved with the development project may be too emotionally involved with the project to be critical of its drawbacks. So an external evaluation is believed to be more authentic by the community. This is particularly useful in assessing the socio-economic impact of programmes. Internal evaluation of course has its own advantage in helping managers of such development organizations in improving overall effectiveness. An important aspect of evaluation is the research methodology which must be decided upon with great precision and in accurate detail, covering parameters of collecting information, methods of collecting information and the sampling plan.

Evaluations are basically impact-studies. In several development projects ex-post evaluation is conducted to determine the impact of the programme in terms of its objectives and goals. The principal aim in such studies is to investigate into the successes and failures of the programme and to delineate the reasons for the same. Consequently, these studies also suggest corrective measures to rectify the flaws.

However, conducting evaluation studies is problematic. It is surrounded by conceptual problems relating to deciding upon the parameters of performance and measurement of variables that contribute to the success. Moreover, there are also problems in it relating to the impacts of the different causal variables.

In evaluation of a project, the 'before and after' approach may be used. Here the impact of a development project is studied by comparing baseline data and post-programme information about the important socio-economic parameters of the beneficiaries. The benefits accruing from the programme may be measured by comparing a scientifically selected 'control' group in terms of those who are covered by the programme and those who are not. In survey research this method is termed as 'with' and 'without' approach, another method is 'action research' where researcher participates in the implementation of the programme.

There are different techniques of evaluation of social development projects—Social cost-benefit technique, PERT, CPM etc. Of these the last two are mostly used for engineering related projects; while the first one, i.e. social cost-benefit technique is widely used for social development projects. As such, the details of this technique are discussed below.

## Social Cost-Benefit

During the last few years there has been a growing necessity for the reassessment of societal priorities and goals in the field of development.

Despite the economic growth in LDC the problems of unemployment, poverty, political and social disaggregation have not been solved. The emphasis has shifted from economic growth to income distribution from production to the satisfaction of human needs, from technology to the development of human resources.

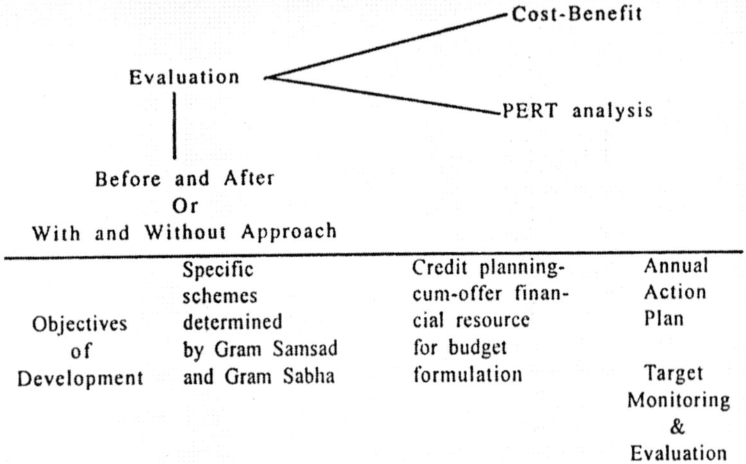


The shift in priorities and the new emphasis on social aspect of development has also called into doubt the usefulness of traditional economic project appraisal and evaluation. To assess the need for new tools of project appraisal-cum-evaluation, it is necessary to determine the differences between the traditional economic projects and so-called social projects.

The social cost-benefit analysis is associated with the methodology of calculating shadow prices to value inputs and outputs of a project, despite the fact that the goal of any project appraisal methodology is to analyse the social cost and benefits of a project.

Costs and benefits cannot be determined in abstract. The costs and benefits of a project can only be fixed within the concrete setting in which the project is executed. The costs and *benefits* of the same project may therefore vary according to :

(1) *The relative factor endowment in the country*

The costs and benefits depend not only on physical and financial factors but also on social, political and cultural constraints, i.e. social cost-benefit technique is widely applicable for social development projects. As such the details of this technique are discussed below.

(2) *The Objectives set by the country*

Since objective setting is a political act and costs and benefits can only be determined according to the objectives set, there is a flexibility in defining the costs and benefits of the project. This flexibility is seldom explicitly recognised.

As economic and social factors are interdependent it will be erroneous to compartmentalise development even for the purpose of analysis. Often economic analysis wrongly ignores the social implications of the project, the social effects and the economic effects being different, it makes sense to distinguish between them.

The economic effect of the project is the effect directly related to the goal of income creation and the costs and benefits of which can be expressed in monetary terms.

Social cost-benefit analysis differs from cost-benefit analysis in so far as the effects of the project are not evaluated according to their profitability to the operating entity but according to their impact on the society as a whole.

Thus the social cost-benefit analysis is similar in form to financial analysis. Both assess the profit of an investment. However, they differ in what they consider as a cost or a benefit. If private benefit would coincide with social benefits there would be no need for distinct analysis. However, for that to be a case, a host of assumptions concerning full-employment competition marginality, consumers' sovereignty, external effects and income distribution have to be fulfilled. Since these assumptions are normally not justified in less-developed countries, social cost-benefit analysis adjusts the final analysis by including (excluding) some costs and benefits which have been excluded (included) in the financial analysis (i.e. transfer payments contingencies, sunk costs, externalities).

Revealing certain inputs/outputs according to shadow prices reflecting their real cost-benefit rather than their market values the social cost-benefits would calculate the opportunity costs, i.e., the marginal output of labour foregone elsewhere because of its use in the project.

The practical existence of difficulties in connection with the social cost-benefit analysis can be due to the calculation of shadow prices. The exactitude of the shadow prices depends on how well the technician translates the subjective welfare function of the decision-maker. The decision-maker can only appreciate the value of the social cost-benefit analysis if he understands the different factors that have been taken into account in calculating the various costs and benefits. The social cost-benefit analysis, therefore, requires a close dialogue between decision-maker and technicians.

The methodology of social cost-benefit analysis can be broken down into the following five stages:

(1) Calculation of financial profitability at market prices;

(2) Shadow pricing of resource to obtain the net benefit at economic (efficiency) prices;

(3) Adjustment for the project's impact on savings and investment;

(4) Adjustment for the project's impact on income distribution;

(5) Adjustment for the project's production or use of goods such as luxury consumer goods and basic needs whose social values are less than or greater than economic value.

Each stage is designed to shed light on the project's desirability from a different angle. No single stage of the UNIDO method can by itself provide sufficient information for judging the merit of a project, for each measures this merit from a different point of view. The decision-makers may wish to take into consideration the following impacts on the project—impact on the financial profits of the investors, on the utilisation of country's resources, on the savings and consumption pattern of the country, on the distribution of income and on any other objectives the decision-makers may wish to take into consideration. Three basic tables can be calculated to get a comprehensive idea of the UNIDO method. The three tables are : (i) the financial income statement, (ii) cashflow statement, and (iii) the balance sheet combined with a few shorter tables used to make adjustment for economic and social values which are the basis for financial, economic and social project appraisal.

In preparing not only the financial income statement but the cashflow and balance sheets as well, a choice must be made between current and constant prices. Forecasts in current prices which include the effect of inflation are necessary to give a current picture of actual financial position of a project in any given year with respect to the costs of inputs and outputs and thus to its cashflow position.

# 10

# FINANCING THE PLAN

## Historical Perspective

The Panchayati Raj System and decentralised governance which are being slowly pushed into the political structure of India cannot be sustainable without financial viability. That is, once a new structure is imposed without fund left to itself it cannot survive for long. For decentralised planning system, i.e., the Panchayati Raj to survive and sustain first of all we need spirited participation of the people and secondly, a stable and steady source of funds coupled with the discretionary right of spending it. Till date this has not been so. However, with the 73rd and 74th Amendments of the Constitution a new scenario is emerging.

The history of the glorious days and later decline of the Panchayati Raj system was well presented by the Ashok Mehta Committee (1978) which identified three phases in the life of this system. These were—the phase of ascendancy (1959-1964), the phase of stagnation (1965-1969), and the phase of decline (1969-1977). Following this last phase pointed out by the committee the decline became more rapid. If we analyse the reasons for this decline and fall we find that hatred and ill-will of the ruling elite towards this institution of self-government was one of the prominent reasons.

In India the British kept alive the working village assemblies and, wherever necessary, these bodies were regenerated. Local self-government, as a representative institution accountable to the electorate was conceived and formed by the British. The important beginning was made in this direction through a government resolution providing for rural local boards with a large number of elected non-official members. In spite of the promotion of rural local self-government by the British only a limited number of villages were brought under the abmit of these bodies when the British left this country. Furthermore, these bodies had only a limited function.

Following Mathew *(Panchayati Raj from Legislation to Movement)* we can point out three generations of panchayats in India. The first generation of panchayats thrived and declined between 1959 and 1977. On October 2, 1959 Jawaharlal Nehru had inaugurated Panchayati Raj at a national rally in Rajasthan. This was immediately preceded by publication of the Balwantrai Mehta study team's report (1957) which advocated the necessity for the community to exercise powers through people's representatives. The golden age of the first generation of Panchayats extended from 1959 to 1964 when they were formed in many places throughout the country. But political leaders and petty bureaucrats were thinking otherwise and the decline began immediately after Nehru's death. From 1964 onwards such antagonistic forces began to expose the shortcomings of the system. They used various means to achieve these ends. One important means was starving the panchayats of funds. Without funds the Panchayats could not perform their most important task of development. This could be done as the control of funds was still not in the hands of these local bodies. From 1964 to 1977 panchayats became an object of ridicule and hatred for those who were, for various reasons, against the decentralisation of power.

In 1977 the Ashok Mehta Committee was appointed. Its report stressed on the need to make panchayats "an organic, integral part of our democratic process". The second generation of Panchayats came into existence when the West Bengal Government, somewhat following the Ashok Mehta Committee report, revitalised the ailing panchayats by holding local body elections in 1978.

In the second generation there was a shift of emphasis from development for the sake of development towards establishment of local governments which functioned as they should. The initiative in West Bengal was followed by Karnataka, Andhra Pradesh, Jammu and Kashmir, etc.

However, the lack of constitutional safeguards inhibited the growth of the second generation of panchayats into truly powerful organisations. Whenever, there was an attempt to devolve power on lower bodies the powers enjoyed by the centre counteracted these measures. So it became clear that any effort of setting up a government below the state had to be accompanied by true federalism at the centre. Yet during the era of second generation panchayats importance of bureaucrats diminished and shifted towards political parties. Also people's participation facilitated through various legislations (lowering of voting age, reservation of seats for SCs, STs, women, etc.) was a marked feature of the second generation panchayats. In the emerging situation a tussel between bureaucrats and non-officials emerged as the bureaucrats were not exactly happy to let their power go.

But as far as finance was concerned true decentralisation was not to be found. Only after the 73rd and 74th Amendments of the Constitution we could hope for some real change in that direction. Before these amendments finance had always been a carefully controlled subject. Though the lower bodies got some autonomy in functioning, the control of finance was always in the hands of the state. So this naturally reduced the process of decentralisation to a farce as funds are most important in transforming ideas to reality. Therefore, local bodies became mere implementers of government projects (poverty alleviation measures like JRY, etc.) and had little say in planning or raising of resources. So they could not function as truly decentralised bodies in the real sense of the term. If they wanted to do so they would be thwarted by vested interests of the state which had the control of funds. Another drawback of the existing infrastructure was that planning did not fully reflect the needs of all people as it was imposed from above. The lower bodies were not allowed to plan for themselves. This furthermore resulted in jeopardising the smooth progress of much developmental work. People at the grassroots level did not have a sense of belongingness. Being mere implementers of projects working with government allocated funds the lower bodies could not feel attached to the development related work that was going on. Moreover, the lower bodies had little or no duties of collecting the funds. They were less careful as to how such funds were spent or whether there was any wastage and corruption or not. What was felt necessary by all well-thinking people was a decentralisation of funds, not mere decentralisation of government powers. Such decentralisation of fund allocation norms for lower bodies entails the right to formulate and implement local area plans. Without this it was impossible to sustain the decentralised framework of government that would slowly come to prevail in this country. This could be ensured only through an amendment of the Constitution, thus making the provisions justiciable and not left at the mercy of self-seeking politicians, bureaucrats and the like.

A new era in the development of Panchayati Raj and urban local bodies (we may call it the era of third generation Panchayats) began to take shape with the passing of the 73rd and 74th Amendments of the Constitution. Now it is felt that lower bodies will no more be at the complete mercy of the state as regards fund allocation, fund raising, plan formulation and implementation. The 73rd Amendment has also laid down that a State Finance Commission be formed in every state to lay down the norms by which fund allocation, fund raising etc. will be organised.

Some of the relevant parts of the 73rd Amendment are produced below :

*Article 243G*

"Subject to the provisions of this Constitution, the legislature of a state may by law endow the Panchayats with such powers and authority as may be necessary to enable them to function as institutions of self-government and such law may contain provisions for the devolution of powers and responsibilities upon panchayats at the appropriate level, subject to such conditions as may be specified therein with respect to

(a) the preparation of plans for economic development and social justice;

(b) the implementation of schemes for economic development and social justice as may be entrusted to them including those in relation to the matters listed in the Eleventh Schedule."

**Eleventh Schedule**

*Article 243G*

1. Agriculture including agricultural extension.

2. Land improvement, implementation of land reforms, land consolidation and soil conservation.
3. Minor irrigation, water management and watershed development.
4. Animal husbandry, dairying and poultry.
5. Fisheries.
6. Social forestry and farm forestry.
7. Minor forest produce.
8. Small-scale industry, including food processing industries.
9. Khadi, village and cottage industries.
10. Rural housing.
11. Drinking water.
12. Fuel and fodder.
13. Roads, culverts, bridges, ferries waterways and other means of communication.
14. Rural electrification, including distribution of electricity.
15. Non-conventional energy sources.
16. Education, including primary and secondary schools.
17. Technical training and secondary schools.
18. Technical training and vocational education.
19. Adult and non-formal education.
20. Libraries.
21. Cultural activities.
22. Markets and fairs.
23. Health and sanitation, including hospitals, primary health centres and dispensaries.
24. Family welfare.
25. Women and child development.
26. Social welfare, including welfare of the handicapped and mentally retarded.

27. Welfare of the weaker sections, and in particular of the scheduled castes and scheduled tribes.
28. Public distribution system.
29. Maintenance of community assets.

*Article 243W*

"Subject to the provisions of this Constitution, the legislature of a state may, by law, endow

(a) the Municipalities with such powers as may be necessary to enable them to function as institutions of self-government and such law may contain provisions for the devolution of powers and responsibilities on Municipalities, subject to such conditions as may be specified therein, with respect to–

  (i) the preparation of plans for economic development and social justice,

  (ii) the performance of functions or the implementation of schemes as may be entrusted to them including those in relation to the matters listed in the twelfth schedule."

**Twelfth Schedule (Article 243W)**

1. Urban planning including town planning.
2. Regulation of land use and construction of buildings.
3. Planning for economic and social development.
4. Roads and bridges.
5. Water supply for domestic, industrial and commercial purposes.
6. Public health, sanitation, conservancy and solid waste management.
7. Fire services.
8. Urban forestry, protection of the environment and promotion of ecological aspects.

9. Safeguarding the interests of weaker section of society, including the handicapped and mentally retarded.
10. Slum improvement and upgradation.
11. Urban poverty alleviation.
12. Provision of urban amenities and facilities such as parks, gardens, playgrounds.
13. Promotion of cultural, educational and aesthetic aspects.
14. Burials and burial grounds; cremations, cremation grounds and electric crematoriums.
15. Cattle ponds; prevention of cruelty to animals.
16. Vital statistics including registration of births and deaths.
17. Public amenities including street lighting, parking lots, bus stops and public conveniences.
18. Regulation of slaughter houses and tanneries.

The 73rd Amendment also instructs the governor of a state to constitute SFC to review the financial position of the panchayats. The SFC has to make recommendations to the governor regarding the principles which should govern distribution of the net proceeds from taxes, duties, tolls etc. between the state and the panchayats as well as the allocation of the same among various levels of the panchayats. The SFC will also make recommendations to the governor regarding the principles which should govern the grants-in-aid to the panchayats from the consolidated fund of the state, measures needed to improve the financial position of the panchayats and many other financial matters of importance. By making the constitution of SFC compulsory powers of panchayats and local bodies as against the state in the area of fund appropriation, expenditure will possibly increase. So the 73rd and 74th Amendments are a great step towards decentralisation of funds and therefore towards true decentralisation.

Hereby we digress to some theoretical matters which deal with the necessity of correct estimates of financial resources at, say district level, that will facilitate financial planning at this level. To do this we have to answer two important questions :

(1) What is the fiscal position of a district ?

(2) What are the revenue requirements of a district ?

Using hypothetical models it can be shown that fiscal position of any jurisdiction is a ratio of fiscal capacity to fiscal need, which is again equal to the ratio of fiscal position to fiscal efforts. While fiscal capacity of a jurisdiction is obtained by multiplying tax base of the jurisdiction by standard tax rate, the fiscal need of the jurisdiction is obtained by multiplying the target population with the cost of providing a standard service level per unit of the population. By dividing fiscal capacity of the jurisdiction by fiscal need we get the fiscal position of that same jurisdiction. Finally, the tax effort of a jurisdiction will equal the ratio of actual revenue in the jurisdiction obtained by applying the tax ratio prevalent there to what would be raised by applying the standard tax rate.

Using another hypothetical model it can be shown that the total financial requirements of a district will depend on the annual growth rate of income of the district, non-plan expenditure or committed liability of the district and the rate of local tax imposed by the district administration. However, in India the annual growth rate of income of a district is assessed by taking into consideration the central sector projects, state sector schemes and district sector schemes. An important conclusion that emerges from the above discussion is that we must be in a position to assess the extent to which the districts are given the opportunity and liberty to take their own decisions related to developmental planning. Again the financial analyst must also know the quantum of resources actually given to the districts and the extent of autonomy enjoyed by them in using these resources strictly in accordance with the requirements of the district plans formulated by the district authorities. In fact, the quantum of resources devolved on the districts, the extent of discretionary powers enjoyed by these districts in the use of such resources and the degree of financial autonomy granted to the districts by the state governments, provide resonably sound criteria for the evaluation of decentralised district planning.

Returning to our original discussion we may recollect that the 73rd Amendment of the Constitution has made it imperative for states to form SFCs which would have to execute various duties. The prime duty of these commissions would be to spell out the principles which should govern the distribution of resources between the state and panchayats and municipalities and also to suggest means through which own resources of these local self-governing bodies may be increased.

In West Bengal the SFC has already been constituted and submitted its report to the government for its consideration.

It can be suggested that the SFC should allow the state to exercise flexibility options in distribution of funds between different local governments. Again in case of West Bengal the proceeds from surcharges on sales tax (which is to replace the abolished entry tax) should go as grants to urban local bodies. From the general trend that has emerged we can distribute the total district plan fund into two parts, grants and entitlements. It can be proposed that the distribution of entitlements should not be left to the discretion of state government. The distribution should instead be according to some fixed norm. Each district and accordingly each sub-unit of the panchayats and the municipalities will be assigned certain proportions of the total amount. Furthermore, our line of thinking is that funds allotted to local bodies should be untied funds. This means that the local bodies should be able to spend the funds as per the priorities that emerge from their own development plans. It will be beneficial for the local bodies if the entitlements granted to them be related to tax collected on the basis of a fixed norm. No arbitrariness can be allowed in this area.

To augment resources of municipalities it can be suggested that the Urban Land Tax and Multi-Storied Building Tax in Calcutta be handed over to the Calcutta Municipal Corporation and this practice should be extended to other municipalities of the state. Then another suggestion is that after tax transfers substantial portion of total net proceeds of taxes of the state collected in a year should be transferred to districts as entitlements. It has been understood that transfer of funds at regular intervals (plan and non-plan) to districts is very desirable for uninterrupted cash flow. Steps should again be initiated so that panchayats can try more seriously to increase their own collections. So should also be the case with municipalities. Another important suggestion is that incentive schemes should be looked into and given importance which will make the panchayats and municipalities more interested to raise their own resources.

Abhijit Dutta (*Finance Commissions and Restructuring of*

*Panchayat Finances*) has suggested some interesting measures in the field of panchayat finance. He has pointed out that the financial jurisdiction of panchayats does not amount to much. This is because the panchayats have a role of maintaining and perpetuating what is executed by higher agencies like the state. Moreover, the existence of state bodies providing parallel local services delimits the functional domain of the local bodies. In this light, the functional domain of panchayats as regards the additional 29 items (11th Schedule) should be spelt out more clearly. Exclusive areas of operation for the panchayats should be made more clear so that their areas of work do not go beyond local jurisdiction. Though some concurrent functions for the panchayat would remain exclusive areas have to be demystified and divided among the various tiers of the lower bodies for better management according to capacity. It has been observed that the panchayats in many states are functioning as little more than agents of the state, more evidently where they are implementers of centrally sponsored schemes. This is a tendency not conducive to the goals of decentralisation. Effective functioning of the panchayats is the final step for total decentralisation. This implies that role of the people can never be neglected. Panchayats should only be facilitators and enabling agents in the process of nation building by the people and private and non-government agents like NGOs. This kind of role is already evident in market-oriented municipal services and in the urban infrastructure where municipal bodies act like a quality control agent and as a protector of the environment.

So the challenge lying ahead the SFCs is not at all simple. They have to clearly enumerate the present functions of panchayats and evaluate the same. After this they will have to make recommendations on kinds and rates of taxes desirable, revenue sharing, volume of grants, etc.

Many problems will naturally spring up. Already it is seen that the states are wanting the SFCs to suggest to the Central Finance Commission (CFC) that the centre should finance the items enumerated in the 11th and the 12th Schedules and that the states do not have to transfer part of their revenues. Therefore, without curtailing the state revenues immediately the money for centrally sponsored schemes on rural development can be channelised to the panchayats.

A look at the 29 items listed in the 11th and the 12th Schedules makes it clear that the income which can be generated from the same will not be substantial. More income generating elastic sources should be handed over to the panchayats so that they might successfuly finance their own plans and be truly viable sustainable people's organisations. Also more avenues for the panchayats to increase their own resources should be explored. Such sources could include royalties on brick fields, earth cutting, sand, etc. Panchayats are better equipped to handle royalty collection of these items.

Decentralisation and devolution of power on the panchayats will naturally entail downsizing of state machinery handling certain functions. If the centre is to share resources (tax revenues) with local governments in a true spirit of decentralisation then a similar cutting down of central government machinery is essential.

Also the SFCs would have to prepare and provide a detailed financial database for panchayats and municipalities. This data will be very important to all concerned with the work of decentralisation.

It has been suggested that in place of setting up SFCs to determine technicalities of sharing from the divisible revenue pool a constitutionally specified formula of entitlements would be a better option. For smoothening the process of fiscal decentralisation tax sharing by the centre would be the best route against any alternative way of achieving similar objectives.

One important area that should not be neglected when going ahead with decentralisation programmes pertains to debureaucratization. As decentralisation will entail some loss in powers of the bureaucracy they will try their utmost to thwart steps towards the full realisation of the goals of decentralisation.

At the Panchayat level bureaucrats working in the field may be absorbed in these local bodies after doing away with excess staff. Then involvement of Panchayat members in executive duties will naturally diminish the need to keep paid government staff to do the same. This and finally the welcoming of non-governmental and private organisations to the process of nation building will naturally make an over-fattened bureaucarcy redundant.

In the area of finance and fiscal transfer the move towards debureaucratisation will be benefited if measures for strengthening panchayat revenue are given priority over executive assistance to Panchayat bodies. Also grants to lower bodies should generally consist of non-salary expenditure items so that panchayats naturally take measures towards debureaucratisation.

A grave danger that may upset the total process of financial decentralisation arises from the fact that lower bodies have very little funds to take up the responsibility vested on them through the 11th and the 12th Schedules. In the late 1950s the Santhanam Committee Report cited five sources of funds for PRIs. These are—

(1) taxes and duties that PRIs can levy,

(2) income from assets,

(3) user charge or service charge,

(4) subventions from the government, and

(5) contributions from public.

However, these conventional sources do not add to much and the gap between income and expenditure of lower bodies remains large and is expected to grow with panchayats taking up certain functions as per the 11th Schedule. So it can be said that PRIs cannot become truly self-financing institutions in the foreseeable future. This is a setback for the process of decentralisation and one economically (though not politically) promising solution seems to be agricultural income-tax. Though unfavourable terms of trade against agriculture are cited as an argument against taking such a measure it has to be remembered that the collected income-tax can always be given back to the local government institutions. It has to be seriously remembered that 30 per cent of the GDP of India (at 1980-81 prices) comes from agriculture and that 10.2 per cent of landholding families account for 48 per cent of India's agricultural land and they do not pay income tax.

Such a situation where agriculture as regards income tax is allowed to remain untouched (except a miniscule tax on agricultural inputs) cannot last for ever. At present, however, self-seeking politicians, the kulak lobby, etc., will thwart any attempt to put a tax on agricultural income. However, in the long run, if we are truly serious about decentralisation and financial sustainability of lower bodies, then all of us have to seriously think about this most promising option with hands on our hearts.

# 11

# GENDER ISSUES AND DECENTRALISED PLANNING

Before going into details about gender issues and its connection with decentralised planning it is important to differentiate between *gender* and *sex*.

While sex is a biological concept, gender is something imposed on (accepted by) individuals by society. In other words, gender is a social construct. Though there are two sexes (female and male) the gender of individuals and their consequent actions depend on social and cultural factors, that vary temporally and spatially.

It is further necessary to differentiate between *gender* and *gender roles* to get a clearer picture of the situation. Whatever gender roles a person may play his or her conception about himself or herself as male or female remains unchanged. This is the gender identity of the concerned person. It is independent of social and cultural structures and even sexual orientation cannot change it. Two males, one who thinks women to be generally inferior to men and another who believes in equal sharing of duties and rewards between men and women, have different gender roles but same gender identities.

In the West gender roles that are presently assumed are the outcome of two contrary forces. These are the coming together of the sexes and the differences among the sexes. In the Western (English and American) societies the first change in gender role between the 16th and 17th centuries was found during the period of Protestant Reformation. The period saw the rise of pre-industrial capital and was marked by a coming together or the stressing of similarities between the two sexes. As feudalism was slowly replaced by capitalism the home and family as centre of religious, educational, commercial activities gained importance and the value and role of women was strengthened.

Again during the 18th and 19th centuries a second change in gender roles became evident. Men were labelled as rational beings while women were said to be emotional.

The structure of the economy was such during that time that women had to withdraw in large numbers from the paid labour force and work at home which became a centre of activity without any commercial value. The appropriate feminine role was motherhood. In spite of the victories of women's libbers and feminists the previous gender roles (18th and 19th centuries) have been somewhat transmitted to the 20th century. However, the nature of similarity of the sexes has not been lost altogether.

From the moment a child is born the gender roles begin to be programmed into the brain. Identification with role models and differential treatment from a very young age serve the purpose of gender role socialisation among individuals.

Men and women have asymmetric access to social rewards. So gender entails inequality. Male dominance shapes culture and is also shaped by it. It unconsciously shapes perception and the day-to-day affairs of everyone who is a part of this culture.

As language happens to be an inalienable part of culture so in a language we also find evidence of male dominance.

Gender issues have no ethnocentricity. They vary depending on culture, the level of a country's development and other numerous socio-economic factors. Gender issues of the first world vary thematically with the nature of the problems of the third world countries. The social condition of contemporary advanced industrial countries significantly differs from the Indian condition. India is, at present, on the path of industrialisation. This recognition of difference and diversity, that women are a heterogenous group divided by class, race and ethnicity; by nationality and religion, by age and sexual performance should be given due weightage to understand prevailing gender problems.

Despite what has been said about women of the world at large they have some common features cutting across culture, race, religion and the level of development.

Women universally are a super exploited under-class. This universality of exploitation of women stems from the prevailing social production. Though the world is mainly dominated by the male, patriarchy alone cannot explain the feature. Patriarchy as a system, following Sylvia Walby, has five important elements like the (i) patriarchal mode of production, (ii) patriarchal relation to paid work, (iii) patriarchal relation in the state, (iv) male-violence, and (v) patriarchal relations in sexuality in cultural institutions. But this alone cannot explain the nature of gender exploitation. In conventional economics, mode of production means production relations—the relation between labour and capital and their respective ownership. Production relations change according to the change in the modes of production, slavery, feudalism capitalism and socialism. Therefore, patriarchy cannot be defined as a distinct mode of production. In every mode of production, excepting socialism, patriarchal elements are present. If socialism as means of production is owned by the state, the production relation becomes gender neutral. In the contemporary world when market economy rules, the prevailing mode is the capitalist mode of production. Under this context we can think of capitalist partriarchy.

The above discussion may be better understood with the help of Weber's classic definition of power. "Power", according to Weber, is "the probability that one actor within social relationships will be in a position to carry out his own will, even against the resistances of others." Here the word 'his' is to be interpreted carefully. Now in this prevailing circumstance one actor within social relationships is the dominant political party or the party in power. Under capitalist mode of production market economy is the economic structure; whereas party system is the political structure. Capitalism works as a result of interactions between the two.

All major political and economic decisions are taken on the floor of the House. Under this system the political party having majority in the Parliament is supreme. Its decisions are carried out by virtue of the majority, be they right or wrong. Again the party structure is such that it is not gender neutral, rather it is gender specific, i.e., male dominated. In this context of patriarchal capitalism the dominant ruling party can be the Weberian "His". Thinking of power from this viewpoint the ruling party has the power to coerce the people to do what they do not want to. There is no scope for discussion and consensus on the issue.

Power and its nexus with the ruling political party has different aspects. The first aspect of power is visible in direct action when force might be exercised on public decisions taken on publicly discussed issues. In the Indian context the classic example is the *Shah Bano* case. The ruling political party in order to appease the Muslim fundamentalists went against Shah Bano.

The second aspect of power can be seen in the attempt to stifle an issue as it emerges; or in the attempt to define or reshape an issue into something less threatening. In India when women on official duty are raped or murdered by the members or sympathisers of some political party, coverage is given as if the heinous act was committed by anti-socials. When a prominent lady political leader while leading a procession is severely beaten in front of police by the supporters of a particular political party with a certain motive, the official version of the report softens the issue as if this was done by the anti-socials with which the said political party has no connection.

The third aspect of power is the hardest to discern. Power, in its third dimension, is used to manipulate people's perception so that they are unaware of having a grievance. The classic case is India's new economic policy with which the country wants to restructure her economy. In all these cases Indian women are the worst victims.

Again deification of the female in the Hindu scriptures does not corroborate with the real social scene in India where women are subject to multifarious deprivation. In the context of family life facile glorification is not only for exploitation in the name of family's well-being but also a cultural concept internalised by women themselves. The women are thus time and again dehumanised.

## Women's Status in Society

The status of women in India is abysmally low. This simple truth does not require detailed elucidation. But a brief statistical discussion on the life of Indian women and the way they are treated will be quite revealing.

The social and economic bases of marginalisation and oppression of women are legitimised by traditional norms, values, institutions and scriptures which provide the broad ideological foundations of patriarchy and casteism. Yet many safeguards were provided in the

Constitution of India to deal with any form of marginalisation, oppression or discrimination. The Preamble to the Indian Constitution resolved to secure to all its citizens justice—social, economic and political; liberty of thought, expression, belief, faith and worship; equality of status and opportunity; and to promote among them fraternity assuring dignity of the individual and unity of the nation. For attaining these objectives the Constitution guarantees certain fundamental rights and freedoms. Indian women should, in theory, enjoy all these rights and perform the concomitant duties at par with men. However, facts point otherwise. Article 14 of the Constitution ensures equality before the law and Article 15 prohibits any discrimination. Again Article 16 (I) guarantees equality of opportunity for all citizens in matters relating to employment or appointment to any office under the state. Moreover, the Indian Constitution empowered the state to make special provisions for women and children.

In spite of these various safeguards of the Constitution, women as a group suffer a lot of social and economic oppression. Upper caste women in small towns and villages of modern India are forced to operate within the limited circle of home-bound activities. The social and economic oppression of women from the scheduled castes and tribes by upper castes is born of intricate entanglements of caste, class and gender forces. In the rural areas and also in large sections of the urban populace women have to bear the burden of housework.

Though no data on India is available regarding the burden of work performed by women, for developing countries taken together 53 per cent of total work burden is shared by women. In developing countries as a whole the average burden of work for women in urban areas is 51per cent and in rural area it is 55 per cent of the total work burden. As regards child labour in developing countries about 10.9 per cent of all girls in the age group 10-14 are economically active.

A person knows oneself primarily through one's body. Other things come later. So assault on or vulnerability of the body indicates a kind of deprivation of the group under question. A woman's body is exposed to vulnerability of many types. Of these female infanticide, sex-determination of foetus and abortion, domestic violence, rape, dowry, murders, etc. deserve special mention.

Another indicator of oppression of women is the cost of

reproduction. It is brought out by the following two facts:

(a) About 80 per cent of pregnant women in South Asia suffer from anaemia ; and

(b) The maternal mortality rate is 460 out of 100,000 live births.

Again home has a special place in the hearts of women but realities have forced more women than men to stay away from home.

Human beings cannot survive without food and deprival of equal rights for food naturally indicates oppression of a class. A variety of factors and practices like male-centred food preparations and distribution, women as second consumer, cultural restraints, etc. deny women equal rights to food. This is revealed partly through the maternal mortality rate.

Education is the external manifestation of the inherent human potentials. In South Asia 50 per cent women as compared to men are literate. Also early marriage variously affects the healthy growth of a person into a responsible individual who can fend for himself/herself. In this sphere we find that 18 per cent of the girls in Asia, 8 per cent of the girls in Latin America and 16 per cent in Africa are married by the age of fifteen.

Employment-wise also, the position of women is not enviable compared to that of men. In the developed countries women occupy 50 per cent of the posts occupied by men. For Africa the percentage is 29 and for Arab countries it is 16. But again employment does not guarantee payment of same wages as men. Worldwide women's pay on an average is 30 per cent to 40 per cent less than that of men.

Again it is a law of nature that women should live longer than men. But in many countries of Asia and Africa due to utter deprivation this natural law has been upset. In India in 1970 life expectancy at birth for females was 97 (index male—100) while in 1992 it has somewhat improved to 100. Yet this is still not in consonance with natural laws.

Deaths related to maternity account for 20-34 per cent of death of women in the age-group of 15-45 years in developing nations against 2 per cent for developed countries.

A girl faces discrimination even before she sees the light of this world. Sex determination tests portray a worldwide phenomenon of preference for the male child. A hospital-based study carried out in India found that only one out of 8000 aborted foetuses was male. The number of females for 1000 males in this country also points to their position in this society. In 1981 there were 934 women per 1000 men. According to the 1991 Census the figure has fallen to 927 women.

In the Indian agricultural economy 75 per cent of the people stay in villages and 70 per cent of the population are employed in agriculture. However, agriculture and allied services account for a paltry 29 per cent of the national income. Landless farmers constitute an important part of this agricultural economy and 44 per cent of them are women. Moreover, 80 per cent of these women labourers are illiterate as against 50 per cent of the men. Also the women labourers are paid less than the men as in other sectors.

Finally, 1991 figures (for India) showing crimes against women present an alarming picture.

In 1991 there was
- one rape every 54 minutes,
- one molestation every 26 minutes,
- one kidnapping/abduction every 43 minutes,
- one act of eve-teasing every 51 minutes,
- one dowry death every 1 hour 42 minutes,
- one act of cruelty against women every 33 minutes,
- one criminal offence against women every 7 minutes.

The above figures for India somewhat broadly outline the status of women all over the world in general and India in particular. The Human Development Report (1997) shows that in 1973 life expectancy at birth for women was 61.4 years (males—61.1 years), their literacy rate was 36.1 per cent (males 64.5 per cent), combined primary, secondary and tertiary enrolment ratio was 47 per cent (males : 63 per cent) and their share in earned income was a dismal 25.7 per cent (males 74.3 per cent). Another important area in India which cannot be neglected while discussing the status of women in politics. Despite their numerical strength women are still marginalised to such an extent because of certain socio-economic delimiting factors. These factors have prevented women from participating in politics in the way men can and have kept them somewhat distant and alienated from the institutional structure of democracy. Political participation includes involvement in any organised activity that seeks to influence or alter the character, function, structure, politics, assignments, behaviour of any institution or power structure in any of the above spheres. This is, moreover, important for women (or for any other repressed group) as it facilitates their empowerment. Here we go about presenting a detailed picture of the political status of women in the world in general and in India in particular. This will complete our picture of the status of women in society.

### *Political Status of Women*

Only 11 per cent seats in Parliaments all over the world are occupied by women and only 6 per cent of National Cabinet Ministerial seats are occupied by them. The number of women in elected bodies all over the world is also much below the desired level. As already mentioned, women have poor representation in the Parliaments around the world, for India the percentage is 7.9. The 1991 census showed that there are 927 women to every 1000 males in this country; however, the female-male ratio as per the electoral rolls is 902 : 1000. This implies that many women are not represented even in the electoral list. Again it has been found that compared to men lesser number of women turn out to vote. The low turnout among women voters can be traced to tradition which holds sway over women in rural areas. Moreover, illiterate rural women are hesitant to vote. These women are not aware of their voting rights nor are they adequately motivated by some other agency to come forward and exercise their franchise. Needless to say, the picture is dismal and much concerted action and participatory work is necessary if things have to change for the better.

These days we have been speaking of sustainable development or rather, sustainable human development. As gender issues, improvement of women's position and empowerment of women is inextricably linked with human development and one cannot go without the other. We must at first attempt to know what human development is. Then we will see the position of different countries as far as human development is concerned. This will be followed by an attempt to define gender development, what it entails and how different countries are placed as far as gender development is concerned. This will give us an idea about the magnitude of work to be done. Side by side, issues regarding role of women in society and the need for their upliftment will be brought to the fore.

Human development is the enlargement of all human choices. Previously, the advocates of economic growth stressed on the increase in income levels only; that is, their focus was on the expansion of only one choice-income. On the contrary human development stresses on the need to expand all human choices, either economic, social, cultural or political.

There is an argument which states that income is a kind of choice which encompasses all others in its fold. That is, expansion of income expands all other human choices. But there can exist an initial skewed distribution of income. For those people who are placed on the lower rungs there would not be much to choose from. Moreover, the trickle-down theory of economic growth may not operate in many situations. Also the effects that economic growth of a country has on its populace depend to a large extent on the national priorities decided by the people or their rulers.

Human development recognises human beings as the ultimate end of development. It has four important components: equity, sustainability, productivity and empowerment.

To grade the position of countries in the area of human development the first Human Development Report was out in 1990. A composite index called HDI (Human Development Index) was prepared for all countries and they were ranked according to this index. The HDI for the latest year (1997) incorporates three important components for each country : life expectancy at birth, literacy (knowledge) and income. So it is in the way of a combination of the GNP measure of economic progress and the Physical Quality-of-Life Index (PQLI).

The value of HDI shows how one country is placed relative to other countries. Countries placed in the high human development group have an overall HDI of 0.907, while HDI for medium human development countries is 0.667. Low human development countries have an HDI of 0.403. The further is the HDI value from 1 (unity) the poorer is the country, region etc. from the point of view of human development. In the HDI tables for 175 countries India comes 138 (in the low human development category with an HDI value of 0.446, Human Development Report, 1997, (UNDP). According to the Human Development Report (1994) India's position in the HDI table was 134 out of 173 countries. This gives us a fair idea about our development.

It is clear that from the point of view of human development we have achieved very little. But HDI does not clearly bring out gender inequalities prevailing in a society. For portraying gender disparities a different kind of index is necessary. Such an index developed by UNDP is the Gender-related-Development Index (GDI). The GDI and the HDI both use the same variables but GDI concentrates on inequality among men and women while at the same time taking note of the average achievements of the total population. The methodology for calculating GDI incorporates the use of a penalty for a country (region etc.) where male-female achievement disparities increase or the overall achievement level of men and women taken together falls. With increasing penalties the GDI falls. So in simple terms GDI is the HDI discounted for gender inequality. As in case of HDI the further is a GDI rank from unity the worse is the country's (region's, etc.) performance as far as gender development (along with human development) is concerned.

In 1992 the industrial countries as a group had a GDI of 0.869 while developing countries had a GDI of 0.560. In a list of 175 countries (HDI report 1997) India has a GDI rank of 118 with a GDI of 0.419.

Finally, the GDI rank of India (in a list of 146 countries) is same as her HDI rank (in the same list of 146 countries) thus implying that investments for development has been irrespective of gender. Moreover, compared to 1970's GDI ranking for 79 countries India's ranking for the same 79 countries in 1992 has fallen by two positions though the index has had a 60 per cent change in value. This implies that within these 79 countries India's relative gender-wise performance has deteriorated in these 22 years.

For ages women, especially due to their physical weakness and a disposition for silent suffering, have been, so to say, under man's feet. Mahatma Gandhi said, "Of all evils for which man has made himself responsible, none is so degrading, so shocking or so brutal as his abuse of the better half of humanity, the female sex. It is the nobler of the two, for it is even today the embodiment of sacrifice, silent suffering, humility, faith and knowledge." He goes on to add, "Women, I hold, is the personification of self-sacrifice but unfortunately today she does not realise what a tremendous advantage she has over man. As Tolstoy used to say, they are labouring under the hypnotic influence of men, if they would realise the strength of non-violence they would not consent to be called the weaker sex. If by strength is meant brute strength then, indeed women are less brutal than man. If by strength is meant moral power, then women are undoubtedly man's superior. If non-violence is the law of our being, the future is with women..." Elsewhere, says the Mahatma, "Women are the companion of men gifted with equal mental capacities. She has the right to participate in the minutest detail of the activities of man, and she has the same right of freedom and liberty as he. She is entitled to a supreme place in her own sphere as man is in his. This ought to be the natural condition of things, and not a result only of learning to read and write. By sheer force of a vicious custom, even the most ignorant and worthless men have been enjoying a superiority over women which they do not deserve and ought not to have."

The father of the nation speaking on the value of procreative act and the service rendered thereto by women says with full sense of responsibility that the mother should know what is her duty from the moment she conceives right up to the time the child is born and she who gives intelligent, healthy and well brought up children to the country is surely rendering a service. Yet sadly, as the later part of this chapter will reveal, government policies and structural adjustment programmes do not attach any value to the time and efforts of women in the maintenance and regeneration of human resources. Throughout our discussions we will be appalled at the glaring gaps between precept and practice, norms and reality.

German philosopher Friedrich Nietzsche in his *Thus Spake Zarathustra* writes with a chauvinistic nuance, "Man shall be trained for war and woman for the recreation of the warrior, all else is folly". Yet he places women on a high pedestal as he describes them to be "illumined with the virtues of a world not yet come". Questioned by an interviewer about the rights of a married woman to own property and the allegation that this may lead to the spread of immorality among women M.K. Gandhi countered, "Has not the independence of man and his holding of private property led to the spread of immorality among men?" In another vein Gandhiji said, "She is essentially a mistress of the house. He is the bread-winner. She is the keeper and distributor of the bread." (There may be some disagreement on this point as winning bread is essential in the present setup for wielding some power in the family or other spheres). He continues, "She is the caretaker in every sense of the term. The art of bringing up the infants of the race is her special prerogative. Without her care the race must become extinct.... There is as much bravery in keeping one's house in good order and condition as there is in defending it against attack from without."

All the advances and victories of women have been won with difficulty. Emeline Pankhurst and the suffragettes, the womens' libbers and the feminists from the days of Betty Friend's *The Feminine Mystique to the Present*, bear ample testimony to that. Yet women's role and importance pervades all aspects of life and living.

The role of women in agriculture was first treated in detail by Ester Boserup in *Woman's Role in Economic Development* (1970). In this book she presented the first ever detailed empirical analysis of women's participation in agriculture. The agricultural systems were classified by her into three groups—female, male and mixed. She showed that in female farming systems women are generally more economically independent and mobile. In male farming systems women enjoy very little independence and are dependent on men for economic support. Again mixed farming system is one incorporating many features of the male farming system and it appears with increasing population pressure on land. Here also women have little independence and they contribute to farming by being employed in tasks like weeding, harvesting and transplanting.

The disappearance of female farming systems has been attributed by Boserup to increasing population pressure on land and introduction of cash crops. These changes began to take place in Asian and African countries in the colonial period. These analyses by Boserup contributed to the building blocks in the process of detailed strategy and research on the role of women as producers, farmers and wage labourers. Further research has dealt with less visible aspects of women's work. Moreover, participation of women in different farming systems was also analysed in detail. These studies found that the contribution of women to agriculture exceeds the estimates of Ester Boserup. It has also been found that women make a large contribution to food production and agricultural wage labour even when they operate in male-dominated farming systems. Also complex relationships between women's role in the market and home fronts and the nature and determinants of women's agricultural work have come to light. Qualified by certain socio-economic and agro-ecological variations it has been found that women are involved in certain particular tasks on the farm. These include growing food for subsistence, weeding, post-harvest storage and processing, small-scale marketing of agro-produce, care of livestock, collection of fuel wood, potable water, etc. However, shortage of farm labour as result of rural-urban migration results in women taking up activities on the farm traditionally reserved for men. Of course cases may arise (Latin America for example) where the rural-urban migration is female-dominated resulting in a shortage of women on the farm. Female labour demand on the farm varies with kind of produce, patterns of land tenure and the degree of integration of this sector with the market driven economy. Studies show that the participation of women in agriculture and their contribution to farm income are higher for small farms which serve local markets as opposed to export markets.

All this is stated here to bring into sharp contrast the gap between roles and rewards that women are forced to bear. Though women participate in such a wide range of activities in the farm sector their access to agriculture inputs is very limited. This results in more labour-intensive work being allocated to women coupled with lesser returns for them. This pattern is more prevalent among female headed farm households with absent spouses. These activities which receive meagre or no compensation, however, contribute a lot to the economy of poor rural households in many countries of the developing world. A country's poverty has been found to go side by side with the number of hours women work and their proportionate contribution to economy and family welfare. Moreover, in developing economies rural women work for longer hours than rural men as well as urban women. Furthermore, activities like collecting water and firewood, sharing and preparing of food for family members, child care, etc. are not accounted for at all (as they constitute unpaid work) in national income accounts and other such measures. Various techniques for measuring these contributions by women have now been devised. A study says that the daily work performed by women which includes household activities, production and marketing ranges from a minimum 5.79 hours per day to a maximum of 12.49 hours per day. In case of men the same figures are 5.11 hours per day and 10.8 hours per day respectively. Again activities related to subsistence performed by the women of poor countries account for 54 to 70 per cent of total household income. Compared to better-off families, earnings of adult women in poorer families are comparatively more important. So it is quite natural that these families near landless and marginal households are more affected by the differential wages of male and female labour because primarily the women of these families work as wage-labourers, artisans, etc. The structure of the household (whether father-headed, mother-headed or jointly headed) also has some effect on women's work. Again the number and ages of children similarly affect their economic participation. Whether women are married or single and their concomitant control over resources have a bearing on their participation in economic activities.

In many places men and boys have greater control over scarce household resources. Women-headed households are generally worse-off as women have limited access over resources like land, cattle, etc. while their economic burden is the same as those of men.

It is possible to comment from the above discussion that for upliftment of women living in villages agricultural projects should basically target small and marginal farmers and should take into account women's role as farmers and resource managers. Such an approach is feasible only under the broad structure of decentralised planning.

We will presently deal with the problem of structural adjustments of an economy in India and what effects such programmes have on women engaged in various activities.

Recent economic liberalisation, instead of ushering a new era of hope for Indian women, has further chained them. Women are universally exploited, but the form and content of exploitation in third world countries varies from those of the first world. The oppression they face is three-fold as they are subjected to race and colour prejudices, patriarchal bias and class exploitation. Hence, production relation under market friendly economy cannot be gender neutral rather it becomes gender specific. After liberalisation leading to globalisation of Indian economy there is a definite tilt towards capitalist mode of production. Therefore the working of economic liberalisation can well be explained under the context of capitalist patriarchy. Under this new mode of production the male-dominated ruling party may manipulate the perception of a near majority section of the population in such a way that they are unaware of having grievances. Taking advantage of their ignorance (which springs from their illiteracy, economic subjugation and other social rigidities is common practice), women who constitute almost half of the population, are not able to perceive their grievances.

## GENDER BIAS IN NEW ECONOMIC POLICY

Four decades of economic planning in India has accelerated growth rate to a modest extent but its development connotation has not gained significant momentum. As a result of that after 45 years of planning we observe that the significant part of our population is still living below poverty line. In terms of HDI index, India's position *vis-a-vis* other developing countries is appalling.

### Reasons for the NEP

Since the inception of planned economic development India opted for socialistic pattern of society and to achieve this mixed economy was adopted as a strategy. Here the Public Sector Undertakings (PSU) were allowed to rise to commanding heights, creating a proper infrastructure for planned economic development. But over the years due to lack of a positive work culture and accountability PSUs have become losing concerns creating excessive pressure on the national exchequer. Fiscal deficit rose to excessive heights and the balance of payments situation was extremely critical. Also, because of high current account deficit and low factor productivity of Indian industries the Indian economy was on the verge of collapse. To salvage India from this critical condition a bold macro-economic adjustment was needed.

Such was the economic condition of India when the Narasimha Rao government came to power in July 1991. The New Economic Policies formulated by the finance minister Dr. Manmohan Singh were directed to restructure the economy to provide a permanent solution to the chronic malaise of Indian economy. The policies introduced in 1991 can be divided into two broad categories. The first set of measures were targeted at short term stabilisation with the aim of controlling inflation and wiping out the BOP deficit. The primary focus of the stabilisation policies is demand management, reducing the fiscal deficit, decreasing government expenditure and rationalisation of subsidies. The second set of measures deal with structural reforms. This is a medium-term policy of rejuvenating and restructuring the economy to ensure rapid growth which is essential for eliminating poverty and establishing social justice.

## Existing Job Scenario of Women

The first set of measures has already set rolling and it is having its repercussion over a wide arena. Among the other things that it will affect is the truth in the saying that gender is a category which will not go away, especially in a country like India. Before launching a discussion on gender bias that becomes obvious in the NEP, we must acquaint ourselves with the present employment situation. 94 per cent of the total women workers are in the informal sector. Working Indian women mainly consist of unskilled labour engaged in the unorganised sector such as salt fields, daily labour, helping hands during sowing and harvesting seasons, tobacco binding industry, maids, bangle and joss-stick, garments industry workers and workers in various other such small-scale industries.

Not only is the disparity in pay between male and female workers (for the same work) glaring but also any form of social security is conspicuous by its absence. For example, in the *bidi* binding industries for every 1000 *bidis* that are bound the female worker gets less pay than her male counterpart. The disparity in pay between maid-servant and man-servant too is glaring. The picture is the same in all the other unorganized or even organized firms where women either get less pay for the same work or the same pay by putting harder labour than her male counterpart. In villages employment opportunity is scarce but the lion's share of the available job always goes to the male. The only reason for this is gender bias. NEP will and is reinforcing the trend of informalisation of the female workforce.

## Effect of the NEP on Job Scenario

The main thrust of the NEP is on privatization. In this new situation where private sector gains momentum disparity between organized and unorganized sector will increase. In India unorganized sector absorbs the majority of the working population, and out of the total employment women-participation figures vary prominently. And women in the unorganized sector have always borne the brunt of an unsympathetic economic system.

It is useful to consider the implication for women in terms of the following variables : access to basic needs, such as food, clothing and shelter and to the provisioning of common property resources; access to education and skill formation which would allow women to move out of low skill and low productivity jobs; access to the requirement of reproduction and nurture of the young including not only health care and other social services but also child care; access to productive employment outside the home and recognition of household work; control over allocation of resources, both within the household and in society.

Each of these is negatively affected not only by the reduction in government expenditure that comes as a part of the stabilisation measures, but also by the general withdrawal of the state from various aspects of the supply of goods and services and the greater reliance on markets which are the desired forms of restructuring of this government. Thus, a cut in public productive and infrastructural investment, such as we have seen in the last four budgets presented by this government, affects not only growth prospects for the future but also production conditions and work situation in agriculture and the unorganized sector as well as in organised manufacturing and services. Cuts in social infrastructure spending have had more effects on living and working condition of women who continue to bear the primary responsibility for household health and nutrition, as well as nurture of the young. They can also affect women's ability to enter the labour market because poverty means an even greater burden of domestic and outside work.

There have been major declines in important forms of public expenditure in real terms over the past four years. The mistake is to see these as 'soft sectors' which government may try to protect solely out of a magnanimous concern for welfare. Experience across the globe has led to the awareness that investment in health education and skill formation is absolutely crucial for future growth and a sound economy. Similarly, expenditure on employment generation schemes has been vital in affecting employment and poverty conditions in the past decade and can go some way in explaining the much wanted improvement in material conditions in the countryside. Declines in real investment in such schemes not only affect employment and incomes but also removes potentially valuable ways of providing more rural infrastructure.

These implications of short-term stabilisation measures are disquieting but they can still be reversed and sufficient pressure can be mounted to ensure that such expenditures are maintained and even increased. However, the likely effects of these liberalisation measures which move towards greater market orientation are even more disturbing, not only because they immediately affect women's material condition, but because they set in motion long term tendencies in the economy, in society and in ideology which is more difficult to reverse. It is often argued that these liberalisation measures are welcome because they will do away with stifling bureaucratic control and excesses with which all of us are only too familiar. But it is important to remember that the alternative which is effectively being posed to this is not the more open and democratic system we desire but a system in which markets operate to the benefit of large, often multinational capital. Such a system is ultimately as centralised, as controlled and as undemocratic, as any that can be imposed by an officious and meddlesome bureaucracy. Because it lacks any form of accountability, it is also less likely to provide economic and social services and rights to those without political clout and financial power. The fundamentally undemocratic nature of the current liberalisation measures is evident from some of the following facts. While rules and regulations are constantly being eased for foreign capital, for FERA and MRTP companies, for large businesses generally and finance capital in all forms, they are still as rigid and restrictive as ever for cooperatives and genuinely democratic alternative organisations. While the overt official assertions speak of the reduction of state intervention, the actual functioning of the state is increasingly becomming more centralised in economic terms. The financial measures undertaken are derived from the policies relating to bank credit which places greater emphasis on capital markets and militates against small enterprises. The focus of labour market reform and the exit policy is on suppression of working class demands and giving greater freedom to fire labour rather than on managerial incompetence and entrepreneurial deception. The point is that this type of liberalisation involves primarily greater freedom of action for large capital both financial and industrial, both domestic and foreign rather than a real liberation of the capabilities of working women and men.

It also entails a fundamental change in the access of women to basic goods and services and affects their rights as workers and childbearers. The main thrust of these liberalisation measures is not only greater commodification of all aspects of everyday life and work, but also a reduction of the subsidisation of activities not valued by the market and a preoccupation with enhancing profitability for exporters and foreign investors through the appropriate manipulation of labour. The inequalising results of the operation of markets are seen as not only necessary but also beneficial in terms of achieving higher growth and greater international competitiveness. The combination of the measures has several very specific effects which act upon the conditions of women in particular.

Since the lives of women are largely governed by the mechanics within the household, their coping strategy has to be seen from two angles. One, the method of coping when the household's well-being is the most important. Often it is this kind of attitude that explains why in the face of inequality and deprivation, women do not protest or question. The lack of a personal perception of welfare combined with a great concern for the family helps to sustain existing discriminatory rules of distribution.

The second dimension of strategy lies in the women having some perception of welfare separate from and perhaps in conflict with the perception of welfare of the household/other members of the household. She then has to make space for herself within the existing distributive rules even whilst attempting to alter them. In this strategy she copes with the intra-household gender specific disparities in distributive rule with respect to income/resource and time.

To go back to the argument about the transition period of the SAP pushing women towards breaking point, the implications of the second dimension of coping on the part of the women raise more questions about the ability of the household to absorb the shocks. Even if one accepts that mothers do not abandon children in times of crises necessity may transfer the burden to more vulnerable members of the household which comprises children, particularly girl-children.

Taken collectively, it seems that the household copes with, survives and absorbs the shocks but the distribution of costs across the members is uneven and the production and maintenance of human resource comprising almost half of the population is jeopardised.

There is an inherent male bias in the formulation of the seemingly gender-neutral macro SAP in that it does not account for the cost and investment of time and efforts on the part of women in the production and maintenance of human resource. The implications of the bias range from a miscalculation of the effects of the macro-policies to a misunderstanding of basic key concepts of the SAP like productivity and efficiency. Further, it has been argued that different policies affect men and women differently. This has not been taken note of by the policy-makers. Since the formulation of the safety net is now a part of the formulation of the SAP the arguments towards engendering policies also extend towards the safety net.

In short the safety net has to be pre-emptive rather than curative or compensatory. It has to serve as a cushion that enhances the survival chances of poor households in a recognition that it is the household that forms the buffer during the transition period. It has to be gender-sensitive in that it encompasses measures which redirect resources directly to women and indirectly through health, education, services, water supplies, sanitation facilities and public transport which then aid them to manage the household as also to participate in market activity.

But available official statistics reveal it is the women in the organized sector who are also being severely affected. The growth rate of women's employment in this sector has shown a sharp decline. The ban on recruitments in the public sector and in government schools has reduced the growth rate from 8 per cent in the 1980s to a paltry 2.7 per cent in 1991-92.

According to the Ministry of Labour's annual report 1993-1994, in 1989, there were 5,19,000 women working in the factories. In 1990 the number decreased to 5,06,000. The number of women employed in mines had dropped from 88,000 in 1989 to 56,000 in 1990. In plantations, which is still one of the major employers of women, the number of women employees had gone down by 2,000.

As a fallout of the NEP, industries are going through closure, sickness and stagnation. The government's target is towards high-tech modernization and subsequent retrenchment. And surely the axe almost always falls on the women first. As a result of mechanization in mines and sectors traditionally employing women, such as coir and tobacco industries, the role of women is being marginalized. A total of 90 per cent of coir workers in Kerala are women and just one machine replaces 90 workers. To cite more examples, women are being marginalized in the handloom and khadi industries; the arrival of business magnets and accomplished entrepreneurs in the fishing industry has displaced lakhs of fisher families. Also the lifting of import restrictions has adversely affected thousands of women employed in silk cultivation. To add more woe to their misery, the job of regular coal mine employees is being made casual. And workers are being relentlessly pushed from the organized to the unorganized sector where working conditions are extremely poor and often inhuman. Moreover, unorganized sector is marked by the absence of any form of support system or social security for its employees. A woman is left uncared for in events such as illness, accident, injury or maternity.

Periodically there is talk of persuading the private sector, especially those enterprises which seek government support, to ensure a minimum percentage of women among the workers. One wonders if the idea has been put into practice. And what sort of positions women, who do manage to enter the organised sector hold? About 57 per cent of them are in community, social and personal services, and 16 per cent in transport, storage, etc.; on the other hand, the government has announced a number of employment and income generating schemes like JRY aimed at providing additional work to the underemployed. But these bring only small benefits to a limited number and have not changed the poverty profile of women. In rural areas 30 per cent to 35 per cent of households are headed by women most of whom are deserted, abandoned wives and widows. They are the sole bread-earners with responsibility to bring up the children.

In such a situation we cannot but remember the words of Klara Zetkin, who pioneered the movement of women's liberation from exploitation, she said that there is a class within class. While bourgeois women fight for their equal right for ownership of capital, proletarian women fight for freedom from economic exploitation of the capitalists.

Elimination of 7,000 licences, scrapping of MRTP limits and

reducing customs duty on capital goods have given free grazing grounds for foreign capital. Following liberalisation of the economy, the right to fish in Indian waters has been given to several foregin firms including Union Carbide. As a result 50,000 fisher folks' families have lost their jobs. Food processing industries with foreign collaborations are being established. There has already been a major shift in the cropping pattern from subsistence production like rice, millet, corn, wheat to cash-crop production such as fruits, mushrooms, flowers, vegetables. This process has affected women's employment in the agrarian sector, as several studies have shown that a shift from subsistence to cash-crop invariably leads to women first losing their jobs. As a result of shrinking self-employment prospects for women a large majority of them join the rural and urban reserve army of labour. The use of women in the informal sector of electronics, diamonds, garments, pharmaceutical industries has increased. Here again, the underlying reality is disturbing. With globalisation of production and introduction of assembly-line production research and management are being controlled by the first world countries while strenuous, monotonous, unskilled or semi-unskilled work is being done by third world women. Lamenting on this situation, the UN Report *The World of Women* (1970-90) states : 'The informal sector is by no means a panacea for women. It is far less secure than formal sector work and it generally pays less than the minimum wage.

Under the NEP women in the organized sector with secured jobs struggle to better their position. However, women in the unorganized sector and those with marginal jobs in the organized sector struggle to keep their jobs. Whoever, had said that the face of poverty is that of a woman was more right than ever as in present times. Not only for the poor but also for the average Indian women to eke out a living is becoming an insurmountable struggle and a battle against gender-bias: the gender-bias of parents at home, of the husband at the in-law's house and gender-bias in government policies.

The pitiable state (with some variations) in which women, who constitute about 50 per cent of the world's population, are placed, of course, warrants concerted action towards their upliftment.

The first step towards such an exercise will be identification of gaps in the general perception of the role of women, both social and economic. Such a study will make it clear that women's labour is assumed not to have direct linkages with the market driven economy. It will follow from this that in many cases women's labour is not monetized and quite often treated as a part or extension of domestic activities. Finally, we will find that the reproductive role of women is not taken in a proper context of development and instead treated with a welfare bias.

We have now seen that women have few opportunities of access to development, resources and services. In general, they are neglected by the extension system and normally do not find a place in its approach contents, infrastructure and target identification parts.

It is commonly believed that the children of a literate mother cannot remain illiterate. So from the viewpoint of making a nation literate it should be a priority that women be taught to read and write. Her education has a kind of multiplier effect on the education of all. Again, literacy and family planning inputs directly affect birth rates and put a check on population growth. This has been exemplified in Kerala and many other places. Population control is the cornerstone of a nation's economic development and women's literacy has a lot to do in achieving this. Similarly, women can disseminate environment consciousness with multiplier effects. The case of joint forest management in West Bengal where women took a leading role can be cited in support of this view. Women being the home-makers can best imbibe health consciousness and inputs relating to nutrition science. This can be achieved by educating them. Such education is best given to women because the multiplier effect (as in all such cases) of educating them is maximum.

It is imperative that a conducive environment be created for total realisation of the potentials of women. This is the key to the sustenance of human beings. Here we have to make an important distinction between mere development for the benefit of women in general and their empowerment.

We will have to create an enabling environment which will be sensitive to the problems and needs of women so that they may be integrated into the development process. It will be necessary for us to study and realize through enabling mechanisms how investments on women for increasing their level of awareness, education, health and for creation of friendly environment for better employment and earning opportunities are essential for improving the quality of life of the family.

Discussion on enabling environments and related mechanisms, naturally, brings us to the concept of empowerment. In short, empowerment is the enabling process of transcending a state of powerlessness. Undoubtedly, empowerment is important for every individual. But it is of greater importance to women who are much more oppressed, than males, as a class due to the male-dominated values of the present patriarchy. Studies have, however, made it clear that a sate of powerlessness, as in the case of women, is not only the result of outside oppression and subjugation by a male-led society but also has some subjective contents. Women are partly powerless because they think themselves to be so. So self-reliance is one of the most important concepts that constitute empowerment. Empowerment shores up confidence and gives a distinct sense of identity for the empowered group. It is influenced by and achieved through the optimum interaction of a number of institutional and social parameters. We can say that while development focuses on the expansion of capabilities empowerment, furthermore, ensures that such created capabilities can be used to take advantage of the opportunities of life. The important distinction between development and empowerment stems from the fact that empowerment and not development is the basic issue in organizing women for their sustainable development. To make a group which is deprived 'developed' has something to do with a sense of condescension and is not sustainable as such. The process of empowerment acts by generating self-confidence and ensures control over resources and the ability to demand and get access to developmental resources. This makes the process of development sustainable. When women become conscious of their rights and are able to face all oppressive forces with courage and determination they are empowered in the real sense. True and sustainable development comes through empowerment. A decentralised planning framework is best suited to go about this difficult task. Grassroots level people's organisations, which constitute the ultimate planning units of a decentralised set-up are most suited to create awareness, give support, and prepare the groundwork for empowerment. Only these organisations are capable of making a woman living in the remotest of villages come forward to participate in the nation building process on equal terms with the male.

The steps for empowerment can be roughly outlined as follows.

*Economic Empowerment by*

(a) identifying potential areas of employment for women and providing the required facilities for imparting qualitatively adequate technical training and skill development in modern technology and processes;

(b) ensure greater access to subsidised credit for taking up of self-employment programmes by educated women, income-generating schemes to supplement the earnings of those women belonging to families living under the poverty line; and

(c) consolidate and expand the thrift-cum-credit groups being formed in villages under various schemes—Development of Women and Children in Rural Areas (DWCRA), Mahila Samriddhi Yojana (MSY) and the like.

*Institutional/Political Empowerment by*

(a) providing information and raising awareness through a process of training on the legal entitlements and government policies at the Panchayat level to enable more meaningful participation of women in local self-government and other statutory bodies;

(b) providing training to women's groups on different programmes and schemes so as to enable them to act as technical resource groups for the elected local bodies to take informed decisions and accord priority to issues that are of concern to them; and

(c) providing 33 per cent reservation for women in the Parliament.

*Social Empowerment by*

(a) providing easy access to women and child health care services, by making available women health providers and strengthening the facilities at the panchayat level through primary health care centres;

(b) provisioning of adequate educational facilities, with particular thrust on education and training of adolescent girls;

(c) provisioning of the supportive infrastructure, with emphasis on ensuring access to fuel, safe drinking water and sanitation; and

(d) establishment of social security system that encompasses specially the care of the aged, destitutes, female-headed households, access to legal counsel, family courts and women-friendly police stations, and government offices etc.

*Cultural Empowerment by*

(a) undertaking training of government and non-government functionaries in gender sensitisation at every important level of interface, with a view to creating right attitudes and responsible behaviour patterns among men and women as it is believed that such corresponding effort in creating social understanding and awareness is necessary to help minimise the vulgarity, violence and the continued debasement of women that is being projected in the media and accepted mutely as the norm; and

(b) undertaking to formulate a media policy that will allot time slots on mass-media channels which will provide access to women and also help create a more sensitive approach to women's issues in the media, etc.

Development with empowerment of women is the new policy that has to be followed and again this can be truly realized under a decentralised planning set-up. The declaration (signed by heads of states and governments) of the World Summit for Social Development held in Copenhagen (March 1995) says,

> "We affirm that in both economic and social terms, the most productive policies and instruments are those which empower people to maximise their capacities, resources, opportunities."

Elsewhere in the same declaration empowerment is brought under a sharper focus,

> "...Recognise that empowering people particularly women, to strengthen their capacities is the main objective of development and its principal resource. Empowerment requires the full participation of people in the formulation, implementation and evaluation of decisions determining the functioning and the well-being of our societies."

The empowerment of women in India leaves much to be desired. The UNDP has devised a measure of empowerment which has been termed (GEM). GEM measures economic, political and professional participation and is not similar to the GDI which primarily measures capabilities and living standards. The power over economic resources is measured using earned income. Access to professional opportunities and economic decision–making is made through a variable in term of women's share of jobs (whether professional, technical, administrative or managerial). Women's share of parliamentary seats measures access to political opportunities and decision-making.

The GEM estimates (Human Development Report, 1997) for 116 countries place India at 101 with a GEM of 0.226 while that of Sweden (placed first) is 0.757. The lesser is the gap of GEM from unity the more is the empowerment-wise performance of the country. The tables for GEM estimates further show that in India 2.3 per cent of administrators or managers are women and 20.5 per cent of professional and technical workers are women. Women's share of earned income is only 19.2 per cent.

However, it is not true that nothing has been done towards empowering the women of our country. State governments and the centre have taken up various programmes from time to time for empowering women. Important ones among these are :

**NORAD and STEP**

These programmes are aimed at women. Under NORAD groups of women are financially assisted so that they might start training-cum-production centres. After completion of training in these centres the women are able to produce for the market. The STEP programme is similar to NORAD but is on a larger scale.

### *Mahila Samriddhi Yojana*

All rural women above 18 years of age fall within the ambit of this scheme. Any woman, living in a rural area, can open a Mahila Samriddhi Yojana account in the post office. The deposits are to be made in cash in multiples of Rs. 4. If she saves Rs. 300 then the Central Government will give her a subsidy of Rs. 75 provided she does not withdraw the money for at least one year. Otherwise she will be provided an incentive @ 12 per cent per annum. As the money is collected in her own account this scheme helps to empower women. She can herself decide on the use of the saved money.

### *Rashtriya Mahila Kosh*

This scheme enables destitute women to get loans for self-employment. The programme also operates through NGOs who take the loan from the *Rashtriya Mahila Kosh* and offer them, in turn, to the needy women. The loans are both short term and long term.

### *DWCRA*

DWCRA (Development of Women and Children in Rural Areas) is another programme with an exclusive focus on women. DWCRA groups operate with a revolving fund given by the government, which is their working capital.

### *Indira Mahila Yojana (IMY)*

A discussion about decentralised planning and gender issues remains unfinished without some comment about this ambitious new project taken up by the Central Government to coordinate and integrate all basic programmes and facilitate their convergence to benefit women.

What IMY basically aims at is an integration of the various departmental schemes aimed at the welfare of women for the express purpose of minimising the lack of coordination when these are implemented through the department. So IMY will function as an umbrella cover aggregating and guiding the smooth execution of all welfare schemes for the benefit of women.

The principal objectives of promoting this new project are :

(1) To ensure convergence of sectoral services at the local, block and district levels, through active involvement of women and sectoral departments.

(2) To optimize the utilization of scarce resources in speeding up the process of mainstreaming women in development.

(3) To create awareness in women through proper flow of information regarding different developmental programmes and issues of specific concerns to women, as also on equality of social status, legal right (like those of property and inheritance), constitutional safeguards. etc.

(4) To initiate a process of awareness generation and education to enable the women to understand and analyse their problems, to find solutions through their collective interaction and to match the individual programme benefits to their needs.

(5) To help women become self-reliant and independent by their economic empowerment through income generation activities and active participation in decision making at various stages.

The three basic constituents of the project as underlined by the Ministry of Human Resource Development, Department of Women and Child Development, Government of India are :

(1) Convergence of inter-sectoral service,

(2) Income generation activities, and

(3) Sustained process of awareness-generation through education.

Two new women's bodies, IMK (Indira Mahila Kendra) and IMBS (Indira Mahila Block Samiti), have been designed as important organisations at lower levels for implementing the project. These bodies would have to be registered under the Registration of Societies/ Charitable Societies Act, thus making them independent of political manipulation. Indira Mahila Kendra (IMK) is the lowermost body to be constituted in the village (*Aanganwadi* level). IMK will comprise a cluster of homogeneous women's groups each group consisting of about 28 to 43 members. Such groups will be constituted on the basis of certain criteria, like felt needs of proposed groups, geographical location, income, education level, etc. There would be some flexibility in such selection criteria. The formation of a homogeneous group for IMK is important *vis-a-vis* DWCRA programme because in the latter, the group which was supposed to be homogeneous actually had leaders of the group belonging to different (higher) ranks of the social order. Again sometimes their names were declared before such groups were constituted. The leader was from a different social strata; no fellow feeling or sense of belongingness developed and the integration of the group was further jeopardized reinforcing the forces of alienation. Formation of a homogeneous group in IMY is therefore a much desired innovation. Initially, the government had launched the IMY as a pilot project for 200 blocks from among the various states and union territories of the country. Each member of the IMK was supposed to make a contribution of Re. 1 per month to the corpus of the IMK. There would be some government grants and grants from cooperatives and business organisations were also welcome. In urban areas IMKs were initially started in municipal bodies having ICDS projects. Members of local Panchayat bodies, post–master, and other such persons were ex-officio members of the IMKs.

The IMKs were supposed to identify and recommend beneficiaries for various sectoral programmes of the departments and such recommendations would be given priority by the departments. Moreover, the IMKs with the assistance of IMBS (Indira Mahila Block Samiti) were supposed to prepare area plans reflecting felt needs of women. IMKs will, moreover, coordinate with the lowest non-political levels of Panchayati Raj Institutions and make the needs of women known to these lower bodies so that these may be considered while formulating plans. IMK being grassroots level organisation set-up as a body through which integrated departmental plans will reach lower level beneficiaries and its constitution as a non-political society furthers the goal of decentralised planning where people's concerns receive focus. In highlighting women, the IMY programme will thus achieve a much needed interface between decentralised planning ideas and the need for women's empowerment.

At the block-level the counterpart of IMK will be Indira Mahila Block Samiti (IMBS). These will also be registered under the

Registration of Societies/Charitable Societies Act and would provide necessary support to the IMKs for group formation resource mobilization, identification of needs and role facilities, etc.

The IMY also proposes to enthuse the IMK groups in taking up income-generation activities utilising group dynamics and influencing various thrift and credit groups to expand their activities.

Again the new project plans to conduct countrywide programmes for generating awareness among women for dissemination of information relating to various government programmes for benefit of women and also to make them aware of their legal rights, constitutional safeguards, etc.

Steering committees at the level of State and Central Government and District Level Coordination Committees (DCCs) under chairpersonship of Collector/CEO/BDO will monitor and integrate activities of IMY at their coorresponding levels. The chairperson of DCC will draw up an annual action plan as IMY.

The 200 blocks that are to be selected for this ambitious project for women's empowerment will have to be ICDS blocks wherein criteria of population below poverty line and high proportion of SCs and STs are included. Moreover, the blocks should also have been selected for EAS and RPDS and there should be a strong presence of an NGO or *Mahila Mandal* working for women and children. The identified NGO will work as a facilitator to the IMBS and help in training beneficiaries, preparing local level project, dissemination of information relevant to women and the like.

In fine, it can be said that formulation of Indira Mahila Yojana is a clear indication that the forces advocating decentralisation and women's empowerment are on the ascendence. The flexibility of IMY to suit local conditions and its emphasis on a need based approach, where the voices of the deprived women at the lower levels will be given due weightage, is a laudable attempt towards fighting poverty and deprivation of women and placing them on equal footing with men in the sharing of opportunities and the successes of life.

Various other schemes and programmes have been taken up which have somewhat served the cause of improving the status of women. Yet much needs to be done as our previous discussions have amply made clear.

The 73rd Constitutional Amendment has provided that one-third of the total seats in panchayat bodies be reserved for women. Moreover, it has been provided in this important amendment that one-third of the offices of chairpersons in the panchayats be reserved for women by rotation in different panchayats. This particular section of the amendment which is basically a move towards decentralisation of powers will facilitate empowerment of rural women. In West Bengal Panchayat elections have resulted in about 35 per cent (reservation is for 33.3 per cent) women being elected for various panchayat bodies.

The section dealing with reservation of seats for women has tacitly assumed an important truth that decentralisation cannot succeed without participation of women. If decentralisation aims at dispersal of power among the maximum number of individuals for their common good then women, who constitute almost half the population, must be included in the programme. Without improvement of women decentralisation cannot take place.

Reservations for women will enable them to take part in planning, implementation and monitoring stages of the people's plan. However, it is often heard these days that women elected to panchayat bodies are surrogate participants in male politics. Such criticisms should not deter us from our avowed goal of decentralisation. Through failures and small advances we will try to give posterity a better day.

Finally in the wake of the 73rd Amendment of the Constitution and the recently introduced IMY project we can mention certain points necessary for holistic development of women. These will receive increased emphasis in the changed situation thus facilitating women's empowerment in the form of decentralised planning.

(i) Women members of panchayats and executive bodies must be adequately trained and empowered so that they might exercise their authority;

(ii) Links have to be established between elected representatives and development functionaries which will enable them to elicit women's participation;

(iii) Trainees and community leaders should acquire interpersonal communication skills. Attention should be focused on training poor women;

(iv) Programmes that are aimed at women must involve and link panchayat functionaries to elicit better women's participation;

(v) Formal representation of women in institutional structures has to be completed by mobilisation of women and involvement of the panchayat in important socio-economic issues that directly concern women;

(vi) Women workers have to be organised (cooperatives, etc.) so that production and marketing could be integrated. Government institutions and welfare organisations should come forward and take up this task;

(vii) Employment should be provided to rural women through activities linked with income generation;

(viii) Conditions facilitating spread of education among women have to be set up;

(ix) Health education, particularly family planning and child care, should begin; and

(x) Proper education in nutrition and other related issues should be imparted to women.

# 12

# DECENTRALISED PLANNING AND ENVIRONMENTAL ISSUES

The happenings of the past few decades have made it very clear to us that the environment is not given to us gratis, that we may exploit and plunder it at our will, utilise and overutilise it trusting it to be a free good, never caring for consequences. We have been taught (though such lessons are only slowly being transferred into positive practice) the hard way that taking the environment for granted is harmful, nay, suicidal for the survival of our race.

It is not to be expected that big capital embodied in multinational corporations will be too eager to pay much heed to environment, unless government compulsions make environment protection imperative. But this aside, there is another important source from where pressure can be created to deal with the problem of exploitation of the environment. This kind of pressure can originate from the local people, who once informed about the dangers to the environment from a project (say), will be most seriously involved in protecting it. They can be the biggest champions for the cause of environment and only a decentralised decision-making system can guarantee that their voices are heard and paid heed to. The resulting process of development will be sustainable.

The importance of environment and its position among the guiding criteria for sustainable development is of recent origin. Environment was taken to be a free good for most of human history. Development dealt primarily with economy and equity. But after publication of the Brundtland Commission Report entitled "Our Common Future", ecology was made an equally important goal of development. The report defined sustainable development as a pattern of development which satisfies needs of current generations without sacrificing the needs of future generations.

The concern for environment is not an alarmist's attempt at sensationalism. The concern is based on real facts, some of which can be noted here.

Of the total potentially fertile land on this planet about 10 per cent has already been turned into wasteland. This is due to interference by or indifference of men. Each year about 8.5 million hectares of land are lost due to erosion of land and silting and again 20 million hectares of tropical forests are cut down annually. The 1980s was the warmest decade of this century and if the global trends of temperature rise continue due to emission of carbon dioxide and other greenhouse gases the sea level could reach dangerous levels causing unpredictable changes worldwide. The danger of ozone layer depletion is looming large. In 1990 OEC nations produced 9 billion tons of solid waste, of which 300 million tons were hazardous wastes. Data of this kind make it amply clear that current patterns of growth still pay little respect to nature. However, our response to such a state of affairs should not be a backtracking which brings us to a position of no growth. Instead what we should aim at, is not to continue previous growth patterns but to develop and put into use new models of sustainable development.

A study has revealed that with the increase in per capita income of a society its use of pollutants also increases but after a certain threshold (of per capita income) the use of pollutants again begins to fall. This fact should be given due consideration while framing policies that lead to sustainable development. The simple solution of maintaining present growth rates and using sophisticated technology to control the damage to the environment does not work. This is so because the better a technology is in controlling pollution the more costly will it be. So it will be more difficult for poor nations to use it. Even rich nations would not be able to sustain present rates of depletion of resources.

The question of sustainability is important and no nation can get away by ignoring it altogether. The faster a nation learns from its past mistakes and does away with unsustainable practices the better it is for its people. If a nation does not change its ways and goes on exploiting resources without caring about sustainability then it may reach a zone of irreversibility beyond which any kind of correcting measures will come to nought.

The Fig. 12.1 makes the above discussion more clear.

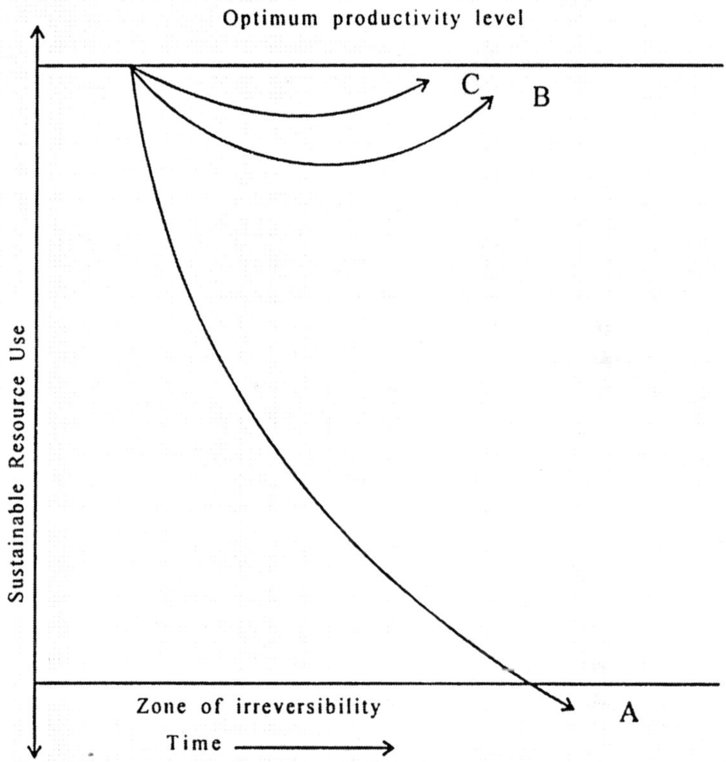


Society 'A' is undergoing a process of unsustainable development, it fails to learn from past mistakes. Society 'C' is making more sustainable use of its resources than society 'B' which is evident from the fact that it takes lesser time than 'B' to correct its mistakes.

**FIG. 12.1**

However, in this context we should remember not to confuse sustainability with the renewal of natural resources only. What is being meant when we speak of sustainability is sustainability of human opportunities. This translates to the sustaining of all forms of capital, i.e., physical, environmental, financial and human.

Decentralised planning, with people's participation through

involvement of local bodies like the Panchayats, is the ideal ground on which sustainability concepts can be nurtured. Only the local people can have the required sense of belongingness to protect the local environment and prevent mindless exploitation.

Once briefed about the dangers of unsustainable practices through examples (like that of boro cultivation and the resulting depletion of ground water levels) local people will be careful that the environment is not exploited and damaged in a careless manner. Techniques of PRD which include TA (Transactional Analysis), PRA (Participatory Rural Appraisal) and AL (Action Learning) can be used to generate this environment consciousness among the local people.

According to Mahabub-ul-Haq sustainability which is the most important constituent of a development package does not imply that all natural resources, all species and the environment should be preserved in the current form. He dubs this attitude as environmental puritanism. Environmental puritanism is not to be confused with true sustainable development. Technological progress, it is hoped, will create substitutes for natural resources and if such substitutes are cost effective and efficient these can be utilised to sustain future human choices.

Environmental protection and sustainable development are ideas very much interlinked with each other. Sustainable development needs sustainable organisations to support it. Sustainable people's organisations like panchayats comprising people from the grassroots level should undertake need, resource and carrying-capacity based planning. They should also seriously take up environmental management and planning while not neglecting common property resources or the important issue of population control. Local bodies can be the best planners and managers of the environment. Being composed of people from the lowermost rungs of the society, these bodies can be most vocal and dedicated in looking after the cause of the environment. The village people live closest to nature and they know best how to take care of it. Only if decentralisation of power and functions gives them ample powers can they take up the cudgels against mindless exploitation of the environment. The panchayats and the administration can play a useful role here by informing the villagers of the various ways through which their environment may be degraded and steps that can be taken to thwart such harmful actions.

With this general idea of how environment is important and what special mechanisms exist in a decentralised planning framework that may keep in check irresponsible exploitation of the same we go on to a more detailed discussion on the importance of environment, and what decentralised planning can do to protect the environment, thus promoting sustainable development.

When we speak of environment we mean all the social, biological, physical and chemical elements that surround us. The environment provides us the resources necessary for our survival and all kinds of enterprises (large and small) continuously interact and work within this environment. Food, energy, water, minerals, air, land, etc. are all provided by the environment. So the resources necessary for living and those required for various kinds of production are supplied by this environment while at the same time it is used as a receptacle for the disposal of waste products.

In the light of our previous discussions regarding sustainability and how local bodies are very important in a decentralised planning framework that strives for sustainable development (Fig. 12.2). It gives a bird's eye view of how a local body like panchayat interacts with various structures that constitute its environment and how environmental management comes into play.

Environmental law, research and studies concerning impacts of various kinds of activities by enterprises can provide useful guidelines for local bodies to follow. In the light of such laws and result of studies they can organise themselves to support or oppose certain practices. Specific guidelines and in-depth studies are of much use when people organised otherwise (from a sense of belongingness for the environment) lack direction to act against the violators.

Environmental law relates the values of a society and resources of nature to the activities of an enterprise. It seeks to define resources in detail covering land, energy, water, minerals, forest, wild life, plants and animals, genetic resources (including their variety), historical resources and cultural resources. Again these laws encourage judicious management of resources generally creating a space for the operation of an environment protection agency which acts as a facilitator in the process. Certain environment related standards and policies are set down by these laws. These laws seek to regulate and limit impacts of certain projects that encroach upon certain environmental systems.

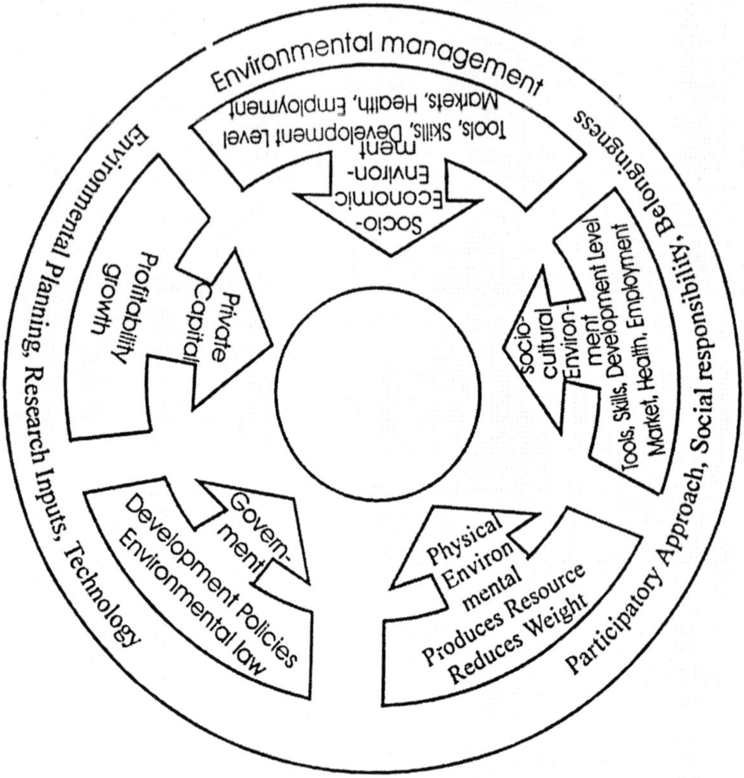


FIG. 12.2: Local body and its Environment

Environment related laws are very often the result of protracted struggles between the government, the polluting enterprises and certain interest groups like NGOs, local people's bodies, etc. NGOs often have a direct and strong influence on local communities and are instrumental in motivating them or in generating a sense of belongingness for the environment. These interest groups can also influence (and are instrumental in the modification of) goals and operations of enterprises by bringing out the nature and details of conflict between the enterprises and its environment. In cases when the local people themselves indulge in unsustainable practices that may be detrimental to the environment (too much use of chemical pesticides and such other green revolution practices) the dissent should originate within them. Else special interest groups or the government can enlighten them of the dangers of such practices and such guidance can go a long way in making them change their minds. However, what is of utmost importance is that people should understand that it is their problem and their sense of belongingness to the environment that should motivate them in changing past habits. Government or special interest groups like NGOs can act only as facilitators in such cases. They cannot dictate the people how to act, the change in perception should develop in the mind of the people themselves.

## Environmental Pollution

The more notable forms of pollution that harm the environment and are thus detrimental to the sustenance of human life and sustainable development are :

### *Air Pollution*

Air is polluted by emissions from power plants, factories, petrol, and diesel vehicles, disposal of refuse and various other means. The most harmful air pollutants are carbon monoxide, sulphur oxides, hydrocarbons, nitrogen oxides and particulates.

### *Water Pollution*

Increased development and growth almost always results in pollution of water. Some of the more important sources of water pollution are:

(1) Industrial effluents which need specialised treatment.

(2) Agricultural sewage which has to be treated specially.

(3) Pollution of inland water bodies by phosphates from detergents and other wastes.

(4) Thermal pollution of water bodies which has much adverse effect on the eco-systems.

(5) Pollution by sewage which affects marine resources (such sewage generally originates from coastal cities).

(6) Industries on the coastline which discharge dangerous toxic substances and also other floating debris into the water.

(7) Oil tanker disasters or solid waste discharges which pollute beaches and affect marine life.

*Solid Waste Pollution*

Inputs of the production system contribute substantially to the formation of solid waste. There can be varied sources of solid wastes. But this kind of waste is very much responsible for various problems. Pollution-oriented solid waste is harmful for humans.

*Noise Pollution*

Pollution due to high decibel levels is a serious problem affecting humans and the environment. Noise pollution can cause heart ailments. High levels of noise in the workplace can impair the hearing of workers and also result in absenteeism and reduced productivity. Noise pollution can cause accidents and is very harmful for ailing patients (in hospitals, for example) and disturbs the peace of offices or educational institutions. Many countries have enacted legislation to check noise pollution. Such laws require employers to provide ear protection for workers. These laws also lay down statutory noise levels for certain areas (inside a city, near an industrial site) and also require that mufflers and other such equipment be placed on machines.

Environmental laws at international and national levels are being framed nowadays to protect the environment from the irretrievable damage by man. Extensive political negotiations coupled with scientific technological inputs go to frame these laws in which a trade-off is made between economic development and protection of the environment.

International environmental law is concerned with–

(a) transboundary pollution (e.g., acid rain) and pollution of marine resources;

(b) pollution of resources shared by two or more states, these may be lakes, rivers or seas;

(c) protection of the international common resources which belongs to no country in particular but to all in general;

Environmental laws framed by particular nations are generally

(a) framework laws which comprise environmental accident prevention regulations, environmental safety regulations, powers and responsibilities of environmental protection agencies, etc.;

(b) conservation oriented laws which are aimed at managing natural resources like forests, wildlife, minerals, etc.;

(c) anti-pollution laws which encompass certain set standards of clean air, auto emission, noise level, zoning regulations, etc.

A somewhat simplified diagram can be drawn to show how a certain project can have complex interactions with the surrounding environment, affecting various eco-systems and human health. The Fig. 12.3 is providing a general idea and particular details will vary depending on the size and nature of the project, the surrounding environment and other specific factors.

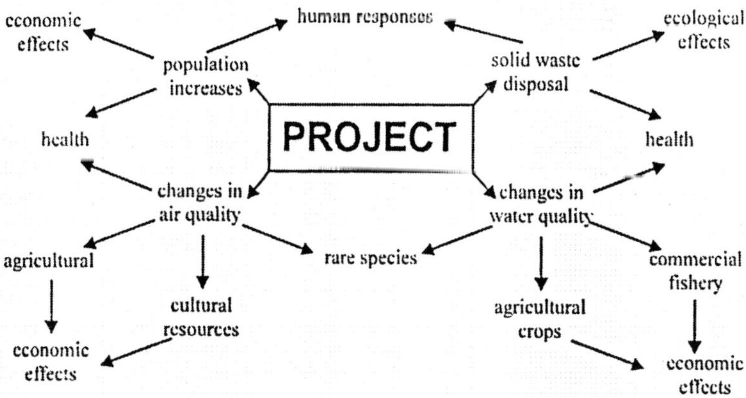


FIG. 12.3

When some new industry is set-up or old ones redesigned Environmental Impact Assessment (EIA) (discussed later) has to be carried out to get a clear idea about how the project will be affecting the surrounding environment. The product policy of an enterprise should be ideally aimed at producing Environmentally Sound Products (ESPs).

ESPs are those products which in none of the stages of manufacturing, selling, use or disposal cause harm to the environment. It may apparently seem that the introduction of some products will be beneficial for the society in general but its environmental aspects should be carefully tested prior to its launching. Such impacts or probable hazards could be inflammability, impact on soil fertility, toxicity, carcinogenous nature, air pollution, water pollution, etc. An ESP in the ideal sense should not adversely affect the environment by any means whatsoever. But it is not possible to design such a perfect environmentally sound product. There are certain criteria towards which the design of an ESP should be geared.

(i) *Overall cost minimisation*—The manufacture and the cost incurred by the society in making, using and disposing of the product should be minimized.

(ii) *Satisfaction of Needs*—The product, depending on its nature, should satisfy needs for shelter, health, food, transport, etc.

(iii) *Beneficial for Society*—An ESP should improve the quality of life and thus benefit society.

(iv) *Quality*—The product should not go out of order and must not become obsolete too quickly. It should have low maintenance cost rather than easy replaceability.

(v) *Resource Conservation*—It should not generate much waste and should be recyclable to a large extent.

When a new project is planned some important questions need to be asked as regards the areas that may be affected. Areas of the following nature have to be given special consideration:

1. Semi-arid areas and desert regions
2. Mountainous areas
3. Coastal wetlands and mangrove forests

4. Natural parks, sanctuaries
5. Tropical and sub-tropical forests
6. Areas of scientific, archaeological or historical interest
7. Areas with a high population concentration
8. Areas for endangered species
9. Places from where vulnerable groups like tribals get important resources.

Decisions of the government regarding projects and various economic policies can adversely or favourably affect the environment. In this context it has to be remembered that there will always remain some areas where government intervention is imperative. This is because such projects (say construction of dams, pipelines, etc.) involve huge amounts of capital and it is not possible to mobilise such huge amounts from micro-levels. In such cases the local bodies can at best act as monitors checking the progress of work and use of public money. The local bodies can also generate public opinion keeping vigil on exploitation of the environment.

Government policies which can have great impact on the environment include changes in agricultural subsidies, alterations in industrial zoning regulations in the outskirts of urban areas. Again widespread changes in land and exploitation of natural resources through wasteland colonization, forest developments, resettlement, minerals development affect the environment; similarly, major irrigation projects, management of river basin including storage and diversification of water, changes in fishing practices have effects on the environment as do projects for development of infrastructure in the form of power plants, railways and roadways.

Finally, the possible impact of the project on environment has to be studied in detail. The various ways by which a project can affect the environment are :

*Socio-economic impact*—Falling standards of living among the poor can start a vicious circle which goes on adding to environmental degradation.

*Land Degradation*—Mindless exploitation by overuse of groundwater or overgrazing results in deforestation, soil erosion, etc.

*Air Pollution*—Industrial discharges and emissions from transport vehicles create air pollution.

*Noise Pollution*—Growth of industry and transport increases the noise level and affects health of individuals.

*Harm Caused to Wildlife*–Forestry resettlement or irrigation projects change wildlife resources. Such damage may affect tangible eco-systems.

This brings us to an important study that has to be done prior to the launching of some new product. This study is called Environmental Impact Assessment (EIA). An EIA deals with the impact of a product on its environment. The following questions are to be necessarily answered through the EIA of a product :

(a) What sort of environmental needs are to be satisfied by the product—physical, social, cultural, etc.?

(b) What are the environmental resources in the form of raw materials, skills, etc. that are essential for manufacturing the product?

(c) How will the physical environment be affected due to the use of the above resources?

(d) How will the use of the product and its maintenance affect the user and the environment?

(e) What parts of the product (inclusive of packaging) may be discarded after use?

(f) How will the components of the product produce an impact on the environment (air, water, soils)?

Before the product is designed an EIA study should be done to facilitate choice of techniques and comparison among alternatives. Similar studies have to be performed before setting up a new industry. On the whole EIA can be described as performing four functions : identifying, predicting, evaluating and communicating concern for the environment.

There are numerous methods that can be used to perform EIA. One of the important and useful methods is the *Matrix method* (Fig. 12.4) that helps to identify specific areas of impact on the environment.

## EIA MATRIX METHOD
## MATRIX-INTERACTION TABLE

***Fill in the matrix by identifying the major impacts of various product characteristics on the environment. Mark (x) for negative impacts, (✓) for positive impacts and (-) for no major impacts.***

| Characteristic / Environmental Areas | Finished product use | Packaging | Transportation | Maintenance | Disposal | Raw materials | Manufacture; Design | Others |
|---|---|---|---|---|---|---|---|---|
| National goals | | | | | | | | |
| Natural resources | | | | | | | | |
| Labour skills | | | | | | | | |
| Energy | | | | | | | | |
| Water Pollution | | | | | | | | |
| Air Pollution | | | | | | | | |
| Soil Pollution | | | | | | | | |
| Solid Waste | | | | | | | | |
| Noise | | | | | | | | |
| Energy needs | | | | | | | | |

FIG. 12.4

The matrix method is shown through the Fig. 12.4.

Following these general elaborations if we look at India we find that the Directive Principles of our Constitution article 48A says that the state should ensure improvement and prevention of erosion of environment. Again Article 51A (i) (g) provides that each citizen should try to prevent pollution and improve the environment including all rivers, water sources, lakes, ponds, forests, etc. in the country.

Broadly four steps can be delineated which are to be followed for environmental viability checking of plans, projects, etc. These are :

(a) Initial Environmental Evaluation,

(b) Environmental Impact Analysis,

(c) Environment Audit,

(d) People's participation in the process.

### The Initial Environment Evaluation (IEE)

The IEE provides a description of the project; of the existing environment and resource use; of potential environment effects on air, water and land thereof; of measures proposed to mitigate or prevent certain anticipated environmental effects; and a judgement concerning the impact of those effects that remain after all known measures for prevention and counter-action have been specified.

At this stage the concerned department should examine possible preventive measures to control environmental damage. These should subsequently be incorporated in the project. The department should also consider those effects on the environment that would remain even after remedial measures are taken.

### Environmental Impact Analysis (EIA)

The EIA exercise that should be undertaken is same as the one discussed in the previous section. This analysis is generally prepared by some consultant who is hired by the department responsible for the project.

**Environmental Audit**

During the stages of project implementation and afterwards it has to be ensured that the environmental standards laid down are being adhered to. In case there is any deviation follow up action should be immediately taken. Any damage or harm to the environment should be adequately compensated in a manner agreeable to the resident population in general in line with the laws of the land. The resident population will know best about the damages and a decentralised system would be most desirable in this context. This is because the voices of the local people will be carefully heard and heeded while environmental audit is done only if a decentralised planning system is in place.

**People's participation in the process**

The local people should be involved in the process from the very beginning. They should be informed in detail about the project and its impact so that they can judge for themselves and take decisions accordingly. Scientific inputs in this case can be very useful. Under a decentralised planning system local bodies like Panchayats, Municipalities, etc. can get actively involved in overseeing the progress of project work and judge about possible consequences for the environment, then or later. This will generate public opinion for or against the project. Local people are best acquainted with local environment and their views, qualified by technical inputs, can be most beneficial for environmental protection and management. Public hearings can be arranged during the formulation or implementation stages. However, public hearings tend to create confusion and smaller groups are sometimes better for the occasion. This area needs further examination and experiment. A viable system needs to be developed where environmental concerns are rightly reflected in project implementation and operation without any kind of bias and without harming the local people whose stakes are the highest. Decentralised planning is a more than correct step in that direction. The views expressed throughout this section have been reflected and developed in an important document that was presented in the United Nations in early 1996 and was later passed in the Rio Conference, popularly known as the Earth Summit. This important document is the *Earth*

*Charter*. It aims to 'enunciate human responsibility towards the life sustaining resources of our planet.' The decentralisation project, it will be seen as we read the clauses of the Earth Charter, will be benefited from and also benefit this project of human care for the environment. The Preamble to the Charter reads:

"We, the people of the Earth, declare that the primary goal of human efforts to put an end to the present destruction of the Earth's ecosystems is to guide and inspire future human development in order to create new life-styles that will guarantee to the whole human population social justice and harmonious relations among nations and peoples and respect for the life giving capacities of our 'Sister, Mother Earth'."

## The Clauses

The Charter declaration contains ten clauses which are :

1. We, the people of the Earth, recognise that human beings are part of and apart from nature. The protection of the environment is essential for human well being and the enjoyment of fundamental rights, and as such requires the exercise of corresponding fundamental duties.
2. We acknowledge that sustainable use of resources requires an effective commitment to the development of a new consciousness and the correction of past errors and inequities, as well as the identification and implementation of new relationships among individuals and human societies and with the Earth itself.
3. We are convinced that the development of just relationship among individual human beings and societies, subject to commonly agreed rule of law, is necessary to the development of harmonious relations with the resources of the Earth.
4. We have acquired the power to modify in fundamental ways the natural systems and life-sustaining conditions of the planet, and do therefore recognise our individual and joint responsibility to understand, respect and safeguard the dynamic processes of the Earth and all that is within its embrace, inanimate matter and all forms of life.

5. We assume our responsibilities for the moral and spiritual order necessary to maintain the life sustaining capacities of the Earth.
6. We, adherents to different religions and philosophies, seek to expand the religious, cultural, and ethical dimensions of human development, and encourage greater cooperation between religious and civil authorities in motivating the most appropriate decisions.
7. We acknowledge that due to harmful activities and lack of foresight, we have created situations that often require immediate redress. All efforts must be made to improve our knowledge of environmental change—local, regional and global—and to develop and use technologies that are compatible with sustainability.
8. We acknowledge the crucial importance of a new understanding of and new options for responsible parenthood to be achieved through education, scientific research and respect for ethical concerns.
9. We acknowledge our responsibility towards future generations by striving to live in harmony with nature. We believe in joint stewardship of the non-living and living elements of the Earth's ecosystem. It is our conviction that this stewardship will permit us to advance towards sustainability for the future, and thus allow for development with equity.
10. We acknowledge that joint stewardship requires all individuals and communities, through their membership in states, to exercise their respective commitments and, consequently, to support other individuals, communities and states in their efforts to do the same.

Following the Charter, a few principles are laid down:

We, the people of the Earth, keeping in mind the above, do hereby espouse and promulgate the following principles:

1. In order to be life-sustaining for present and future generations, the resources of the Earth–air, water, land, flora

and fauna—must be protected by all states and peoples.

2. Inasmuch as the life-sustaining systems of the Earth are either altered or influenced by human choices, humans must strive to work towards equality, the just distribution of this world's goods, and a healthy and productive life by peaceful means in harmony with nature.

3. Insofar as states possess the sovereign right to develop their resources, they are also responsible for preserving the environment and the quality of life of their own citizens as a universal good, and for avoiding damage to the environment of other states.

4. In order to advance towards a pattern of sustainable development, humans must responsibly use renewable resources, safeguard those resources that are not renewable, and above all, eliminate overconsumption of all resources.

5. Inasmuch as the unprecedented growth of poverty and the unequal distribution of wealth and major causes of environmental degradation are concerned, all peoples and governments are responsible for combining their efforts to eradicate poverty, this being an essential requirement of sustainable development.

6. In order to assume fully our stewardship, the cultural, moral and spiritual development of persons and communities must be given greater emphasis so that the Earth may ever more become our common home. May the realisation of these principles be inspired by the ideals of Saint Francis, the Little Poor Man of Assisi, in whose simplicity of life-style we find riches for the proper attitude towards our 'Sister, Mother Earth'.

# 13

# EVOLUTION OF NGOs AND ITS IMPACT ON DECENTRALISED PLANNING

Whenever the state (nation) moves away from areas of operation certain spaces are created which other bodies or organisations can fill up. With the backtracking of the state as a consequence of decentralisation many such organisations are naturally found to become active in different fields of work with the aim of national welfare. These bodies may voluntarily spring up as a natural consequence of the state's withdrawal or they may be deputed organisations that the retreating state leaves behind for the welfare of her people. Non-governmental organisations can easily fit the description of the first kind of organisations while local government institutions like panchayats are institutions of the second kind.

The relation between state and voluntary organisations has seen the whole gamut of possibilities from partnership to outright offence. Though the government is often portrayed as a monolithic structure with uniform policies at all levels, in reality there may be different reactions from the government's side according to the level concerned. If a generalisation has to be ventured then it can be said that the relation between NGOs and the higher bureaucracy ought to have been on the whole neutral. However, in the recent past we have found that some NGOs have been blacklisted on corruption charges which naturally implies a clear nexus between them and the higher bureaucracy. One trend lately visible is the utilisation of voluntary agencies by international organisations for distribution of international development aid. It is an interesting observation that international organisations which are in reality associations of governments find their views matching with small voluntary groups which are struggling against their respective national governments. Presently a positive approach is being tried by both national governments and NGOs who are trying to come closer to one another by breaking the negative stereotypes that each possesses about the other. Yet conflicts remain. NGOs harbour doubts about the avowed impartial nature of the state. Again, the complaint against such voluntary organisations is that their cost efficiencies have no solid basis. But this does not, of course, show the bureaucracy in a better light because it is anybody's guess whether the perk-enjoying bureaucracy is cost-efficient.

In the context of decentralised planning coupled with the structural reforms and adjustment programmes that have been taken up by the Indian government, the role of NGOs becomes more important. Structural reforms naturally entail some displacements, population migrations, loss of work for people and other similar social hazards that have a wide and deep impact on the population. It is not possible and practicable for the state to take care of all these. It is more so because NGOs and private bodies can better manage these problems. NGOs are better equipped to handle situations that demand item-wise response rather than the generalist response that the state can manage. NGOs, because of their more professional attitude, are more suited to tackle whatever tasks are given to them while the executive bodies of the state and their employees being paid government servants with secured jobs tend to be lackadaisical, unconcerned and corrupt. Decentralised planning which naturally depends on wholehearted people's involvement can benefit much from NGO's activity. Government servants tend to have stereotyped ideas about villagers and think them to be lazy and lacking dynamism. Moreover, they somewhat correctly think that villagers always look upon the government as givers and themselves as mere receivers of public goods and have an utter sense of distrust in their own ability to do something. Again, villagers harbour negative stereotypes about government servants. Only if Panchayat officials and people from the grassroots level work hand in hand, each sharing their strengths and nullifying their weaknesses can decentralised planning be a success? To achieve this end NGOs can assume the role of facilitators and enabling agents who act as a mediator between these parties and also enthuse people to get involved in the nation's work which is actually their own. If NGOs responsibly take up their role of trustees to the funding organisations (as envisaged in Mahatma Gandhi's thought) and look upon their work as developmental, not as an alienating service that pays profit but as an important work of nation building then their role will be more appreciated and the country will reap greater benefit from them.

Kerala State Planning Board has come out with a novel idea of VTC (Voluntary Technical Corps)–"A comprehensive list of potential retired and non-official experts in the state is being prepared. Any expert who is willing to spend at least one day a week to render voluntary help to panchayats will be enrolled in the VTC." The response is quite encouraging. For participatory planning, role of NGOs is very important in resource mapping, need identification and monitoring and evaluation. This has been successfully experimented in South India.

## The History

Before the nineteenth century voluntary action in India was mainly evident during natural disasters like floods, famines, etc. Other than these, religious groups took part in voluntary activities for welfare of the people. A system of *madhukari* was prevalent in parts of the country during this time. This was a system by which poor brahmin boys had arrangements with certain households from where they used to get regular meals. Again historical evidences seem to suggest that there were certain organisations in India which took up such activities like planting trees on the roadside or digging wells.

The medieval period also saw prevalence of the practice of constructing *dharamsalas* for travellers. This practice still remains in this country. Mutual interests played an important role in focusing the direction of voluntary action in medieval India. It helped to keep poverty in check but systematic efforts for the mitigation of suffering in the face of natural crises were lacking. Then again caste and religion played an important role in the channelising of voluntary action, thus somewhat diluting the benefits obtainable from it. During the 19th century the religious reforms, reforms in the social structure and also social work on a voluntary basis made their presence felt. In this context eminent personalities like Raja Rammohan Roy, Dababhai Naoroji and others are worth mentioning. In the late 19th century western enlightenment ideas coupled with eastern thinking made their appearance through the work of great leaders. Thus grew up important organisations which took part in social reconstruction and voluntary action like Ramakrishna Mission, Arya Samaj, Bharat Sevasram Sangh, Anjuman-Himayat-Islam, etc. Christian missionaries also did much work mainly by setting up orphanages, old-age homes, etc. Secular organisations also took up this task in later times.

Religion as the driving force behind voluntary action began to become less important in the early 20th century and was replaced by reason. Mahatma Gandhi arrived on the scene during this time and his simple life and high ideals influenced hundreds of people to voluntarily take part in social welfare programmes and in the removal of evils of the system. In 1937 Mahatma Gandhi established the Harijan Sevak Sangh which was totally dedicated to the welfare of Harijans. This organisation is working till today.

An important change in the field of voluntary action began to be felt in the early part of the 20th century. What had begun as a disorganised and unstructured activity began to get a form and direction. Organisations dedicated totally to voluntary welfare activities began to get registered. These organisations were not all religious as before and they were not always working to engage with the powers that be in their welfare-related activities. There were many reasons behind the change in voluntary bodies from disorganised units to organised structures. The social awareness of national leaders, the spread of education, breakdown of traditional institutions of social security, changes in the expectations of a section of the population, refugee rehabilitation after the country's partition and many other factors contributed to this change. Areas of voluntary action that have received maximum stress from the beginning till date are welfare of women, the handicapped, the destitute and children.

There is no precise estimate of the number of voluntary organisations registered in this country. Between 1947 and 1971 about 10,000 such agencies were established all over the country. People's participation had always been a part of voluntary action programmes but policies of the government and its assumed role of a giver have somewhat nullified the enthusiasm of the people in nation building work.

No uniform pattern of growth is seen in the establishment of voluntary organisations. It can be said from reliable estimates that immediately after independence and the following years there came into existence many such organisations. Concentration of such organisations is most evident in the states of Maharashtra, West Bengal, Gujarat and Kerala. A large number of voluntary organisations in this country is to be found in the west followed by the east. One important matter that needs to be highlighted is the fact that such organisations have tended to focus on developed areas because of better infrastructural facilities available there. Thus, economically weaker areas have remained weak and neglected.

Distribution of voluntary organisations in the country has been secured for other reasons also. Varying levels of literacy and the prevalent socio-political scene have been a contributing factor. Also accessibility to power centres and men who can get work done have generally resulted in these bodies being set up in towns, state capitals and metropolitan cities. It is being easier to recruit men and obtain material and resources in urban areas the voluntary organisations have tended to concentrate in such areas. This is not at all expected especially after a decentralised system of governance comes to prevail in the country. The decentralisation project aims at an equitable distribution of resources, both intra- and inter-generational. However, if voluntary organisations concentrate on certain areas this goal is defeated as they happen to be an important organ through which decentralisation is made operational. Again there are instances where people have come out on their own to participate in order to solve their own problems without much external assistance. *Chipco Andolan* (embracing of trees to prevent their cutting down) in the Garhwal region of Uttar Pradesh or the *Mitti Bachao Abhiyan* in Hoshangabad of Madhya Pradesh or *Narmada Bachao Andolan* are some such examples. Such movements will receive greater impetus if scientific knowledge channelled through voluntary organisations is made available to the involved people. Thus their work can get a much needed direction. NGOs are much better organised and are theoretically less biased and possess superior technical expertise that make them ideal in this above mentioned role of facilitator, motivator and provider of information.

As regards programmes of the voluntary organisations a new approach has made its presence felt in recent years. This is the replacement of an institutional approach of solving problems, a broadbased integrated system of action. Decentralised planning aims at balanced all-round development and its primary aim is to reflect everybody's needs in the formulated plans. An integrated approach is best suited to deal with this demand whereby synergic results are obtainable. So the switchover from the institutional towards integrated work of voluntary organisations is welcome in the context of decentralised planning. Similarly ad hoc measures have been replaced by comprehensive and systematised programmes and stress on research and survey has been emphasized. Research impacts as discussed elsewhere are very important for the smooth working of decentralised planning programmes in areas like plan formulation where agro-climatic features are to be known beforehand.

NGOs should be the organisations of choice which are handed over projects of the government. Being non-profit organisations they are preferable compared to contractors who always have an eye on profit. Also government contractors will ultimately be an instrument of the government bound by its laws and rules, while NGOs can work in a more independent manner, more conducive to decentralised planning goals. The volume of work that the government has in its hand cannot be handled by itself alone. Moreover, with decentralisation many state functions are coming in the hands of panchayats and such local bodies which are not equipped to perform the same. In this situation taking NGO's help is imperative and in a choice between government contractors and NGOs the latter should be preferred.

However, this chapter does not intend to be a through and through advocacy of NGO activity. We should be careful that NGOs do not become small bureaucracies with their own hierarchies and power centres. Then the object of involving them in nation building would be defeated. And more transparency should be brought into their functioning so that the non-profit nature does not remain non-profit in letter only but in spirit also. For 'the letter killeth but the spirit giveth life'.

# 14

# PLANNING PROCESS IN WEST BENGAL

To trace the course of development of the planning process in West Bengal we must go back to the pre-independence days. During the British period some acts were formulated by the rulers of the country with the express aim of strengthening foreign rule. These acts were in no way meant to enable local self-government establish itself in the country.

The first such act was the Bengal Chowkidari Act of 1870. This was followed by the Bengal Local Self-Government Act of 1885. This act resulted in the formation of district boards at the district level and local boards at the sub-divisional level. Local boards were later on done away with and the *Thana* level union committees were formed. The Bengal Village Self-Government Act was formulated in 1919 which resulted in the creation of district boards and union boards. No further acts were formulated prior to independence.

After independence Balwant Rai Mehta Committee Report had far-reaching implications towards establishment of grassroots level organisation and decentralised planning in the country. The committee recommended that three-tier panchayat system would be suitable for the country. Following its recommendations a four-tier Panchayat system came into being in West Bengal. The two relevant acts were West Bengal Panchayat Act, 1957 and the West Bengal Zilla Parishad Act of 1963. The four tiers were the gram panchayat at the village level, *Anchal* Panchayat comprising a group of villages, the block level *Anchalik Parishad* and *Zilla Parishad* at the district level. Only at the Gram Panchayat level there was a provision for elections.

The three-tier Panchayat system which one finds in West Bengal at present came into being after the West Bengal Panchayat Act, 1973. Following this general elections for all the three tiers had been held in 1978, 1983, 1988 and 1993. These three-tiers that now exist are the Zilla Parishad at the district level, the Panchayat Samiti at the block level and the Gram Panchayat at the village level.

The system of elections that was initiated for all the three tiers ensured greater transparency within these organisations. Other than these three bodies mentioned there are two other non-political bodies at the lowest level below gram panchayat. These are the *Gram Sabha* and the *Gram Samsad.*

Gram samsad is the lowest non-political body of the people comprising all people in a single polling booth whereas gram sabha comprises all voters.

The lowest elected body of the three-tier panchayat system is the gram panchayat which has between five and twenty-five elected members. The elected head of the Gram Panchayat (GP) is called *Pradhan.* Local members of next higher body, Panchayat Samiti are ex-officio members of the Gram Panchayat. Just above the Gram Panchayat is the Panchayat Samiti (PS) which is the people's elected body at the block level. It has under its jurisdiction a number of Gram Panchayats. The elected members of the PS come from the different *grams* under its block where a *gram* as notified by the government comprises a single or a group of *mouzas.* One *gram* can send at most three elected representatives to the PS. The ex-officio members of the PS comprise pradhans of the GPs under the PS, local members of the Zilla Parishad excluding *Sabhadhipati* and *Sahakari Sabhadhipati* and also local MLAs and MPs. The chief of the PS is called *Sabhapati.* He is the elected head. The executive officer of the PS is BDO while the Extension Officer of the Panchayat (EOP) is the secretary. Again services of all staff working for the block have been placed at the disposal of the PS. The highest body of the three-tier Panchayat System, i.e., the body at the district level is the Zilla Parishad (ZP). The ZP constitutes elected members where each block (PS) sends two members to constitute it. District MLAs and MPs and *Sabhapatis* of the Panchayat Samitis falling under a particular district constitute the ex-officio members of the ZP. The elected head of the ZP is called *Sabhadhipati* while the district magistrate of the district is the executive officer. An officer of additional district magistrate's rank is same as additional executive officer and an officer of the state civil service has the role of a secretary. Technical persons like executive engineers, assistant engineers, etc. work with the ZP.

This is the overall structure though it is debatable whether this structure at all exists and if so, how efficiently it functions in the state in the task of formulating a decentralised plan. We will discuss later how in spite of giving people's organisations the power to spend funds after the 73rd and 74th Amendments of the Constitution there still remains coordination problems between Panchayat members and administrative and/or the department offices. The overall control of development activities has been given to the people by giving the *Sabhadhipati* of the Zilla Parishad the status of minister-of-state. He is also the chairman of the district planning committee (the executive and planning body for the district with statutory powers) as well as various other committees through which the panchayat system functions.

A somewhat similar structure is also found at the block level.

The Panchayat System of the Panchayati Raj Institution functions (formulation, execution of plans, etc.) through ten permanent committees both at *Zilla* (district) and Panchayat Samiti (block) levels. These committees are called *Sthayee Samitis.* The ten *Sthayee Samitis* are :

(1) *artha, sanstha unnayan-o-parikalpana* (finance, establishment, development and planning)

(2) *Janaswasthya-o-paribesh* (public health and environment)

(3) *Purta karya-o-paribahan* (public works and transport)

(4) *Krishi, sech-o-samabay* (agriculture, irrigation and cooperative)

(5) *Shiksha, sanskriti, tathya-o-kriya* (education, culture, information and sports)

(6) *Khudra silpa, tran-o-janakalyan* (small industry, relief and welfare)

(7) *Bon-o-bhumi sanskar* (forest and land reforms)

(8) *Matsya-o-prani sampad bikash* (fish and animal resources development)

(9) *Khadya-o-sarbaraha* (food and supplies)

(10) *Bidyut-o-achiracharit shakti* (power and non-conventional energy)

The chairman of a standing committee is called *Karmadhyaksha*. He is elected from amongst the members. However, in case of finance, establishment, development and planning the *Sabhadhipati/Sabhapati* is the chairman ex-officio.

The standing committees have ex-officio members, nominated members and elected members. In case of the committees at the ZP level the ex-officio members are the *Sabhadhipati* and *Sahakari Sabhadhipati* while for the standing committees at the PS level *Sabhapati* and *Sahakari Sabhapati* are the ex-officio members. The elected members, between three and five in numbers, are selected from the members of the ZP and PS. Government officers, eminent persons with specialized knowledge and such other individuals are the nominated members of the committees and they are selected by the state government.

So it is clear that these ten committees are the most important bodies as far as planning and other functions of a panchayat are concerned. With decentralised planning making some headway in this country and getting a further boost after the 73rd and 74th Amendments of the Constitution, the powers and functions of the panchayats in the villages and municipalities in cities and towns have increased. The above two acts have spelt out a number of areas (29 for panchayats and 18 for municipalities), the planning functions relating to which will be under the jurisdiction of these local bodies. Moreover, the 73rd and 74th Amendments of the Constitution have directed that State Finance Commissions be set-up in each state which would suggest ways and means for delegating financial powers to panchayats and municipalities and would recommend devolution of resources from the state level to the local levels. In West Bengal a SFC has been constituted and it has already submitted its report and recommendations which have been heartily accepted by the cabinet. However, no attempts have been as yet made to put these recommendations into practice. Out of the 29 items suggested by the 73rd Constitution Amendment over which panchayats have total financial and planning jurisdiction, 17 have been accepted by the West

Bengal Cabinet. According to section 207B (amended in 1994) of the West Bengal Panchayat Act, 1973 the state government may transfer any or all of these 17 items mentioned below to panchayats:

(i) Agriculture including marketing and food processing

(ii) Irrigation, minor irrigation and water management

(iii) Animal resource development

(iv) Health and family welfare

(v) Public health, engineering and rural water supply

(vi) Social welfare

(vii) Land and land reforms, land improvement

(viii) Cooperative

(ix) Khadi, cottage and small-scale industries

(x) Rural housing

(xi) Public works and communication

(xii) Education

(xiii) Fisheries

(xiv) Social and farm forestry

(xv) Rural electrification

(xvi) Poverty alleviation programme

(xvii) Public distribution system

That this state is slowly moving towards decentralisation is clear from the fact that many of the above functions have been and are being handed to the Panchayats. However, maximum decentralisation has occurred in centrally sponsored projects like JRY, IRDP, RWS, etc. very recently all self-employment schemes like IRDP, DWCRA, etc. have been clubbed together and renamed as Swarna Jayanti Rozgar Yojana, and all wage-employment schemes like JRY etc have been renamed as gram Samriddhi Yojana. Execution of these projects has been handed over only to panchayats, but lower bodies have been mere implementers and spenders of government money. No feedback from them regarding local conditions and aspirations of the people have been thought necessary.

The following is a summary of recommendations made by the SFC. It is followed by an item-wise note on the decisions of the cabinet regarding individual recommendations, whether it is accepted, rejected or is under consideration.

SUMMARY OF RECOMMENDATIONS

1. Local Self-Government (LSG) institutions will not be able to discharge their responsibilities without adequate funds and staff. As things stand now, they will have to depend heavily on grants-in-aid and sharing of taxes with the state government and on the continuation of grants from the union government through poverty alleviation and other schemes. This report has suggested ways to give the local bodies more powers.

**Grants-in-Aid**

2. Over the past decades, the proportion of plan expenditure for districts has increased and with further decentralisation, this share will go up. A substantial part of this should be entitlements to the local bodies in the form of untied funds and the rest will continue to be grants.
3. Our proposals on modification of some grants to municipalities need mentioning. In place of entry tax, a surcharge on sales tax has been introduced. As promised, the state government should distribute the fund to the municipalities as grants in the same manner as done so far with money from the entry tax. State grants on parts of collection of profession tax and motor vehicles tax to LSGs may be discontinued.
4. Since price rises are not within the control of the municipalities D.A. subventions to them should cover the whole of the D.A. liability in respect of approved staff. Further, since various benefits to the staff have been introduced at the instance of the state government, it should

cover such expenses with grants.

5. A large number of centrally sponsored programmes such as JRY, IRDP, ARWSP, etc. are now in operation in which the central releases have to be matched by proportionate state releases. Such state and central releases would continue to be grants and will not be part of the untied entitlement of the local body concerned.

**Tax Sharing**

6. Entitlements will be financed by sharing of taxes. In lieu of sharing individual taxes, 16 per cent of the net proceeds of all tax collected by the state in a year should be transferred to local bodies. These will be untied funds at the disposal of the local bodies. Such funds may be released to districts in suitable instalments, quarterly or monthly.

**Devolution of Taxes**

7. Taxes on entertainments, now collected by the state, should be handed over to local bodies.
8. Urban land tax and multi-storied building tax should be handed over to Calcutta Municipal Corporation.
9. Collection of irrigation rates along with the related responsibility of water management and routine maintenance be handed over to concerned Zilla Parishads.
10. Resources generated in a regulated market should be brought within the purview of DPCs and the net proceeds ploughed back in the market hinterlands.

**Own Incomes of LSGs**

11. The West Bengal Panchayat Act has empowered the three tiers of Panchayats to raise taxes, levies and tolls from a wide range of fields. These efforts should be stepped up.
12. Fiscal powers of LSGs have been set forth in various legislations, but further spread is necessary. Rules have to be

framed and clarifications to be given in some cases.

13. Periodical assessment by the Central Valuation Board (CVB) should be made mandatory and the CVB strengthened adequately for this purpose.
14. The state should take up with the Union Government for timely payment of service charges for Union Government properties.
15. Municipalities should be empowered to issue trade licences with fees at a much higher level; to impose tolls at higher rates for heavy vehicles on municipal roads; to impose levy on tourists/pilgrims; to impose water tax on large users and commercial and industrial undertakings; to introduce special conservancy charges for commercial and industrial establishments.
16. There is considerable scope for increasing non-tax revenues.
17. Voluntary contributions have been made a notable feature in the development activities of the panchayats and this should be encouraged to garner more resources as well as to enhance people's participation. Municipal boards may also try to involve the people to improve urban facilities.
18. Incentive schemes have been suggested to encourage panchayats and municipalities to increase their own incomes. Two per cent of entitlement due to a district will be set aside to operate an incentive fund.

**Adjustments in District Organisation**

19. Transferring of a few hundred crores of rupees to districts as entitlements will inevitably affect the present organisational set-up. Supervision of the departmental staff, remittances of non-plan expenditure to districts and breakdowns in the state budget will have a new look.
20. Tax collection in the state should also adopt a new approach. The state tax collecting officials will work in cooperation with LSG functionaries. The existing Decentralised Resource Mobilisation Scheme will no longer be necessary but the

existing incentive scheme for small savings should continue.

**Planning**

21. District Planning Committee (DPC) has now been given constitutional status. In this state for nearly a decade planning committees were functioning at the district level. But the planning process needs to be much more comprehensive. Also the process should start at the GP level and move upwards with appropriate modifications at upper levels including the State Planning Board.

**District set-up**

22. The three tiers of panchayats and municipalities will get money from three sources, own income inluding donations, entitlements and grants from the state and the centre. The first two sources are untied and local bodies will be free to spend them according to their chosen priorities.

23. The projects formulated by GPs will be usually small and technically simple which may be executed with local expertise. Larger schemes will have to be vested with the PS.

24. Maintenance of assets created so far in blocks will be the prime responsibility of PSs. They will also have assigned responsibilities.

25. ZPs will have a greater scope to create new assets and to concentrate on more complex types of maintenance. Besides, as the apex body in a district, it will have various coordinating responsibilities.

26. Maintenance and development in towns will be done by municipal authorities with the help, when necessary, from the ZP and the state.

27. A few districts have some inhabited areas which are outside the jurisdiction of panchayats and municipalities. These have been termed as special areas in this report. These areas will also be allotted funds in proportion to their population and

the earmarked funds will be operated in consultation with the DPC.

28. There are development boards in a few districts besides the panchayats. Funds for their operations will come from the state and not from the entitlements of local bodies.

**Distribution of Entitlement Funds Amongst LSGs**

29. The entitlements suggested in this report do not depend on accretion of additional funds but are only a redeployment of funds which are now being spent in the districts. Instead of basing the distribution on population sizes only a few factors indicating backwardness have also been taken into account, so that backward localities may get proportionately more money. The selection of indicators depended on the availability of reliable data. The entitlements in the tables have been given in percentages.

30. For distribution among districts the factors taken were population, level of non-literacy, proportion of backward population, area of the district, proportion of rural population and inverse ratio of per capita bank deposits and of working capital of primary agricultural cooperatives taken together.

31. Within a district its allocation should be divided among panchayats, municipalities and special areas on the basis of respective total population.

32. The distribution among municipalities has been based on certain factors like population, level of non-literacy, proportion of SC/ST population and population density.

33. Of the total entitlements going to panchayats the proportional allocations among three tiers are : ZP—30 per cent, all PSs put together—20 per cent, all GPs put together—50 per cent.

34. The distribution among GPs has been made on the basis of population, level of non-literacy and proportion of SC/ST population.

35. The distribution among PSs has been based on the same three factors as in case of GPs.

36. Due to the special constitutional status of DGHC, the commission has not earmarked its entitlements futher amongst municipalities, panchayats, etc. For Siliguri sub-division, the Siliguri Mahakuma Parishad has been playing the role of the ZP and has been treated accordingly.

**Other Points**

37. The Tenth Finance Commission has recommended certain grants for the local bodies of the state over and above the devolution recommended by the State Finance Commission. Such additions should flow to the districts so as to be available for use by the local bodies.
38. Works under the state plan sector and district plan sector should be clearly listed by the state government.
39. Departmental maintenance budget should be disaggregated district-wise and communicated to the districts. DPCs should be involved in supervising maintenance works.
40. In the proposed new set-up, the burden of work of *Sabhadhipati, Sahakari Sabhadhipati* and executive officer will increase considerably. Sharing of work with chairpersons of standing committees will be essential. Similar distribution of work in lower rungs will also be necessary. Cooperation of departmental staff will also have to be mobilised.
41. Block level staff of different departments have already been placed under concerned PSs. However, some confusion is still prevailing over deployment of such staff and this should be resolved immediately.
42. The question of regularising excess staff in municipalities was examined according to certain norms by the Second Municipal Finance Commission. The state government should examine the recommendations and take a final view.
43. Auditing of incomes and expenditures is a must for healthy running of local bodies. Suitable and adequate number of persons from existing employees in the district should be selected for the job who will be fully engaged in this work. No additional recruitment should be necessary.

44. There should be some effective penal provisions for local bodies not falling in line with financial discipline. Penal measures are also to be introduced for those municipalities which divert development grants to meet revenue expenditure.
45. A new standing committee (*Sthayee Samiti*) may be created in each ZP to help develop favourable milieu for small-scale and large industrial units.

## EXPLANATORY MEMORANDUM AS TO THE ACTION TAKEN ON THE RECOMMENDATIONS MADE BY THE WEST BENGAL FINANCE COMMISSION IN ITS REPORT SUBMITTED TO THE GOVERNMENT ON NOVEMBER 27, 1995

1. The Report of the West Bengal Finance Commission (hereinafter referred to as the Commission) constituted under Notification No. 1023-FB dated the 30th May, 1994 together with the Explanatory Memorandum on the action taken on the recommendations of the Commission is being laid on the table of the House in pursuance of Article 243-I(4) and Article 243-Y(2) of the Constitution of India. The summary of the recommendations of the Commission relating to devolution of state taxes, grants-in-aid and other matters is contained in Chapter 7 of the Report of the Commission. Along with the summary of the recommendations. Chapter 7 of the Report also contains some observations of the Commission. The decisions of the Government on the recommendations of the Commission are indicated in the following paragraphs.

**2. Grants-in-aid**

*Recommendation 2* : This has been accepted by the Government.

*Recommendation 3* : Surcharge is a part of sales tax and sales tax including surcharge is to be taken into account for the determination of entitlements as per recommendation 7.07. As such distribution of surcharge on sales tax separately to the municipalities is not necessary, the recommendation that state grants in lieu of collection of profession tax and as assignment of part of Motor Vehicles Tax to local bodies may be discontinued has been accepted by the Government.

*Recommendation 4* : The Government has accepted the recommendation in respect of approved staff subject to review in due course on receipt of the recommendations of the 4th Pay Commission.

*Recommendation 5* : The Government has accepted the recommendation subject to the decisions that may be taken by the Government of India on the question of transfer of Centrally Sponsored and Central Sector Schemes to State Government.

**3. Tax Sharing**

*Recommendation 7* : The principle that entitlement of local bodies should be financed by sharing of taxes has been accepted by the Government. But this has to be related to recommendations 7.39 and 7.40, i.e. clear listing of the works under the State Plan Sector and District Plan Sector and district-wise disaggregation of departmental maintenance budget for which detailed exercise is being done in consultation with Administrative Departments.

**4. Devolution of Taxes**

*Recommendation 8* : This is being examined.

*Recommendations 9 to 11* : These recommendations have been accepted by the Government.

**5. Own Incomes of LSGs**

*Recommendations 12 to 19* : The Government has accepted these recommendations in principle. The details are being worked out.

## 6. Adjustments in District Organisation, Planning and District set-up

*Recommendations 20 to 29* : The Government has already accepted this approach in general. Details will be worked out in due course.

## 7. Distribution of Entitlement Funds Amongst LSGs

*Recommendations 30 to 37* : The Government has accepted these recommendations.

## 8. Other Points

*Recommendation 38* : The Government has accepted this recommendation.

*Recommendations 39 and 40* : These have already been dealt with.

*Recommendations 41 and 42* : The Government will take a view as recommended, while undertaking the exercise for implementation of recommendations 7.39 and 7.40.

*Recommendations 43 to 46* : These will be considered in due course.

Where implementation of any recommendation of the Commission as accepted by the Government requires enactment of a law by the State Legislature, necessary action for introduction of such legislation will be taken in due course.

An important step towards decentralisation of planning, powers and functions was taken in this state by forming the District Planning Committee (DPC) and the Block Planning Committee (BPC). The DPC and BPC were formed in 1985-86 with the *Sabhadhipati* of the ZP as the leader of DPC and *Sabhapati* of the PS as the leader of BPC. The members of the BPC are like department officers at block level, *Pradhans* of GPS and *Karmadhyakshas* at PS level. The BDO is the member-secretary. Similarly, DM is the member-secretary of DPC and it is constituted of *Sabhapatis* of Panchayat Samitis, chairpersons of municipalities, district level line-department officers and *Karmadhyakshas* at ZP level. However, only recently the DPC was made statutory through the West Bengal District Planning Committee Act, 1994 with far-reaching implications for decentralised planning in this state.

The methodology of decentralised planning followed presently starts with informing each district of the budget allocations of different departments for that district. The sum total of these allocations for a district is called the *district divisible pool.* The DPCs then have to prepare the district's plan on the basis of this district divisible pool. Utilising the various committees the districts prepared their plans and similar actions were undertaken at lower levels like block/municipality. A system of prioritisation of needs elicited from people at grassroots level is supposed to be used to formulate plans at the lowest level and in a bottom-up manner these plans will be sent to the next higher level till all such individual micro-plans accumulate (after prioritisation) to give rise to the total district plan. In West Bengal we have only managed to achieve this; though we are much ahead of other states. If the expenditure can be cited as a measure of decentralised planning then the following statistics can be cited :

**District Divisible Pool**

| Year | Budget allocation for districts (In lakhs) | Percentage |
|---|---|---|
| 1987-88 | 34262.39 | 39.75 |
| 1988-89 | 41495.31 | 43.64 |
| 1989-90 | 52984.66 | 47.52 |
| 1990-91 | 65538.91 | 49.35 |
| 1991-92 | 76087.07 | 51.20 |
| 1992-93 | 82234.44 | 55.78 |
| 1993-94 | 91809.00 | 59.23 |
| 1994-95 | 101251.16 | 61.00 |
| 1995-96 | 117583.96 | 53.27 |
| 1996-97 | 154429.82 | 50.12 |
| 1997-98 | 1197729.01 | 49.66 |

To ensure that planning is totally decentralised and bottom-up in nature the West Bengal Panchayat Act, 1973, as amended during 1992-94, has some important sections, namely 16A, 16B and 17A which state that GPs are to formulate plans and implement the same after consultation and discussion with people at meetings of the two non-political lowermost levels of the panchayat, namely *Gram Samsad* and *Gram Sabha.*

Sections 16A, 16B and 17A state:

Every GP shall hold an annual meeting in May and a half-yearly meeting in November for each *Gram Samsad* for discussion on the budget, draft plan and audit report of the GP. The GP shall, on collecting the information about *Gram Samsad*, place it before the *Gram Sabha* in December for its deliberation and recommendations. All these recommendations are taken into account for the purpose of formulating annual plan and deciding the mode of implementation of programmes. The Gram Samsad may act as guide and adviser to the GP in regard to the schemes for economic and social development undertaken or proposed to be undertaken.

As far as development planning for municipalities is concerned the relevant act is the West Bengal Municipal Act, 1993. This replaced the Bengal Municipal Act of 1932. An 'area development' concept had been introduced in the 1993 Act. This concept generally deals with renewal of already developed areas and is silent regarding taking up new areas for development.

The Act of 1993 spells out that the goverment of this state can declare an urban development region of a municipality which may comprise municipal jurisdiction, as its urbanised growth area. The municipality, it has been said in the Act, will prepare master plan for upgrading of the human settlement within such region. Again the Act states that the government of this state can constitute urban development committees for any area or areas outside the municipal area for the purpose of implementation of a master plan. The board of councillors of the municipality shall have to consult the urban development committee in all matters of preparation of a master plan and also its implementation as far as they relate to areas outside municipal area. All planning and development activities in an urban development region have to be carried out under the overall supervision and control of the board of councillors of the concerned municipality. Another important Act that will have some bearing on the municipal planning taking shape in this state following 74th Amendment of the Constitution is the West Bengal Town and Country (Planning and Development) Act, 1979. According to it a planning area has to be declared with the urban and local bodies as the planning authority which will prepare ODP and DDP following the provisions of this Act. But with the introduction of the 1993 Act it seems that the WBTAC (Planning & Development) Act, 1979 will be restricted only to Calcutta metropolitan area.

It is clear from a perusal of the two Acts specially in case of the 74th Amendment that these are confusing and how municipal planning will take place remains an open question. In this context it is notable that no urban development region has been as yet declared in this state so as a result no urban development committee could be constituted or a master plan prepared.

The 74th Amendment was a bold step towards decentralisation of municipal planning. A direct fallout of this amendment in West Bengal was the West Bengal District Planning Committee Act, 1994 through which DPC was constituted. The main function of the DPC is to formulate draft development plans for the district and the metropolitan areas. As per Article 243ZD of the Constitution the DPC would be consolidating plans prepared by the Panchayats and the municipalities in the district and this provision is also embodied under Section 10 of the West Bengal District Planning Committee Act. Similarly, as per Article 243ZE of the Constitution, the Metropolitan Planning Committee would also prepare plans for areas falling within its jurisdiction. This has also been embodied in Section 3 of the Metropolitan Planning Committee Act, 1994. In case of the district (excluding metropolitan area) the system of decentralised planning that will be followed is somewhat clear and has been discussed before. However, for municipalities and for the district (excluding municipalities) little progress has been made and a lot of confusion exists. The WBDPC Act, 1994 says that each municipality is to prepare annual plans and programmes of execution for five years. These plans and programmes will be examined and finalised by the urban developer's sub-committee for consideration and inclusion in the draft development plan for the district by the DPC.

In a manner similar to the bottom-up planning set-up being tried out by the panchayats, the municipalities have also had to create ward committees as dictated by the 74th Amendment to facilitate such planning. The ward committees are the lowest formational constituents of urban local bodies and have important responsibility in the field of planning and execution. These responsibilities are either obligatory or discretionary; they may be functions transferred by the state government. Thus urban people, through the ward committees, can directly participate in the planning process and thus the cause of decentralised planning will be validated. The government of West Bengal has taken important initiative in the formation of these ward committees and these steps have made West Bengal an example among other states moving towards decentralisation. In spite of such hopeful news the move towards decentralisation of planning in urban local bodies falls far behind what has been done in the Panchayats. The 74th Amendment has listed a number of items that will be under the total jurisdiction of urban local bodies and from which these bodies will have to raise resources and plan execution. However, all this is yet to take off and presently the fund raising method of urban local bodies is under consideration.

We can only wait and hope that a parity between urban and village planning is reached in the near future and the overall tempo towards decentralisation is maintained in good spirit aided by spontaneous participation.

# 15

# AGRO-CLIMATIC REGIONAL PLANNING AND DECENTRALISED PLANNING

In the agricultural sector growth was first 'area-led' and later on 'technology-led'. In the last four decades of planning in this sector the very important issues relating to land, water, rainfall, climate, etc. were kept in the background. It was only in the late eighties that a realisation dawned upon scientists and planners that something must be done immediately to reverse the trend of soil depletion, salinity and waterlogging, falling groundwater levels and deforestation by large scale use of modern technology and soil nutrients. The result was concretisation of the concept of Agro-Climatic Regional Planning (ACRP) by the planners and its adoption by the Planning Commission as a national planning methodology in 1988. For the first time natural resources and environment were given explicit recognition and agricultural planning was sought to be designed within the framework of homogeneous Agro-Climatic Regional Planning. In brief ACRP means identifying homogeneous agro-climatic regions and formulating integrated development plans for such regions with stress on ecology, economy and equity. With this broad idea in mind the country was divided into 15 agro-climatically homogeneous zones and 75 sub-zones for formulating ACRP based plans.

### Essence

(a) ACRP is a distinctive planning approach applied to agriculture and allied sectors.

(b) ACRP is essentially resource-based planning. All other parameters or features associated with ACRP are either derived from this essentiality or are incidental to it.

(c) ACRP is not limited to the dimensions of crop sector alone. It includes the entire range of land and water resources based activities covered under the broader definition of farming systems.

(d) ACRP approach seeks to achieve the best trade-off between maximisation of productive efficiency of given resource endowments through use of appropriate technology and institutions and long-term sustainability of such resource use both in the sense of maintaining inter- and intra-generational and social equity in the access to resources.

(e) ACRP approach combines area-based planning (as against sectoral or schematic) in a holistic manner.

(f) ACRP is not to be confused with decentralised planning, though ACRP approach becomes more relevant in a decentralised planning framework. Unlike before ACRP provides the much needed technical input to the decentralised planning process.

(g) ACRP approach encourages adoption of regionally differentiated strategies based on integrated area-based solutions rather than generalised macro solutions. At the same time it tries to achieve a balance between the local and regional/ national priorities.

(h) ACRP approach is based on the principle of convergence of resources and funds from different sources like the goverment, the financial institutions and beneficiaries.

(i) ACRP encourages innovative research and strategies and provides a forum for interaction/feedback between scientists, planners, administrators, bankers and beneficiaries.

(j) ACRP approach leads to building replicable models under similar sub-regional homogeneity.

(k) ACRP approach puts emphasis on building data and information base at the district level using modern information system for giving the required technical content to district planning.

(l) The ultimate aim of the ACRP approach is not to build a new typology of plans but to enable the district planners to internalise and institutionalise the idea of ACRP.

**Objectives**

ACRP is a conceptual bridge between resources and decentralised planning which aims at sustainability in relation to land and water-based agro activities. ACRP implies that future agricultural development programmes are required to be specific to the regional development strategies which will not be the prototype extension of the existing programmes. ACRP aims at more diversified agricultural development which would concentrate on afforestation, animal husbandry, agro-based industries, pisciculture, etc. The main objectives of ACRP are :

(i) to prepare land and water resources based strategy,

(ii) to examine crop and non-crop based development opportunities as component,

(iii) to formulate for a resource base a plan of crop and non-crop system,

(iv) to develop investment plans for the above,

(v) to examine phasing and feasibility question and operational viability,

(vi) to evolve detailed institutional, marketing and infrastructural support systems.

The following may be considered as the concurrent steps that could be taken for achieving the desired results within the overall principle of ACRP:

1. Organised area based approach for land utilisation and modification of cropping systems.
2. Judicious exploration of ground water resources and optimum harnessing of surface water.
3. Development of appropriate husbandry for rain-fed

agriculture.

4. Poverty alleviation programmes for a region should be compatible with the factors of production locally available.
5. Streamlining marketing system to avoid monopoly of unscrupulous traders.
6. Development of agro-processing industry for economic use of surplus agricultural produce by forming farmers' group cooperatives.
7. Introduction of high value crops in relatively plain areas to act as vegetative barriers.
8. Water impounding structures like percolation tanks, dugwells and *nalabundhs* should be introduced in porous formation to conserve surface run-off water.
9. Promotion of natural vegetation through agro-forestry, social forestry, minor fruit trees, alternative conservation measures like contour trenches are to be adopted to restrict soil erosion.
10. To the extent possible water bodies should be utilised for culture of quick growing fishes and upgradation of existing animal resources should be taken up by involving landless labourers and small and marginal farmers.
11. Development of agro-based industries.
12. Impart training through demonstrations, farm trials and field visits.
13. Undertake various research activities in the field of soil and water management, crop improvement, animal science and also region specific research for optimal utilisation of resources.
14. Undertake concurrent monitoring and evaluation of the project, suggest remedial measures and mid-course correction, wherever and whenever necessary.
15. Encouraging the active participation of panchayati raj institutions, NGOs and line departments, keeping in view the necessities of the people residing in various project areas.

All this, as already mentioned, has given birth to the concept of

ACRP which the Planning Commission wants to institutionalize all over the country.

The emphasis in this institutionalisation exercise is on absorption/ assimilation of the ACRP approach in the existing planning system. This consists of two important elements, the supplementing of the exisiting planning machinery with technical and research inputs and intense interactions with existing organisations and training-orientation programmes.

Institutionalisation of ACRP is intended to internalise the experience in terms of approach and application pertaining to land and water related activities within the existing/emerging planning and development system in the country. With the passing of the 73rd and 74th Constitutional Amendments and its confirmation by all the states a new direction and sense of priority has been imparted to the institutionalisation exercise. Considering the approach provided in the 73rd and 74th Amendments ACRP perhaps provides the building block between the decentralised planning process and scientific resource-based planning process.

Considering its basic rationale and thrust the work planned in related states consists of :

1. policy level assessment and commitment in adoption of the ACRP approach by the state,
2. setting of interface among various departments.
3. training orientation of government functionaries,
4. setting up of core planning committee to work as integral part of district planning process,
5. setting up of planning and information bank, and
6. exchange visits.

The logical but important extension of institutionalisation relates to integration of the ACRP plan with infrastructure development plan and convergence of ACRP plan with the poverty eradication and social development programmes. The Planning Commission has made a provision for technical and financial support to states as per requirement schedules to accomplish the process of institutionalisation leading to the total adoption of the ACRP approach.

In this context two important decisions taken during the seventh annual meeting of ACRP at Kodaikanal (June 1995) deserve special mention. These are:

(a) establishment of the ACRP Documentation and Dissemination Centre (ADDC) at Ahmedabad, and

(b) setting up a core group for institutionalisation of ACRP during the Ninth Plan.

The important task of the ADDC is to disseminate technical, scientific and strategic information generated by the ARPU (Agro-Climatic Regional Planning Unit) and other related agencies to a variety of clients. It will involve multimedia and GIS to enhance the effectiveness of planning and implementation of development projects using ACRP approach.

Here it is pertinent to mention that though ACRP is chiefly concerned with agriculture yet under this kind of planning agriculture has been given a holistic view incorporating all primary sector activities, including agro-processing industries. On the whole ACRP will try to balance local and regional/national priorities. It will try to provide technical inputs to the decentralised planning system, provide for implications relating to support systems, and last but not the least will be aiming to balance short-term and long-term goals of development. Decentralised planning speaks of the bottom-up approach to planning where the felt needs of the people from the grassroots level are assessed and necessary planning is done after prioritisation through the three-tier panchayat system. ACRP is also a grassroots level planning process where the agro-climatic variations among various regions are taken into consideration.

The scenario that will emerge in case ACRP is successful is one where power will be totally decentralised and the goal of empowerment of the lowermost classes will be reached.

The main objectives of decentralised planning need to be mentioned in this context. It strives to increase production through efficient utilisation of local resources, which includes absorption of modern technology. It seeks to generate employment opportunities particularly for agricultural labourers, rural artisans, small marginal farmers and other weaker sections. Moreover, it aims at removal of poverty and improvement of living conditions of target groups at the same time keeping in mind equitable sharing of benefits of development both among the people and the regions. Hence a comprehensive decentralised planning policy should bring the ACRP approach within its ambit.

# 16

# PROBLEMS AND PROSPECTS

The government of the country is making it apparent that it is serious, at least in letter, about decentralised planning or the grassroots approach. But in the complex socio-political milieu of this country with the power nodes pulling in different directions and other vested interests in constant operation what we ultimately get is still in the realm of conjecture. What we can best do in the present juncture is to clearly underline the main problems so that when obstacles come in our path we may be ready to deal with them.

If decentralisation is reached at least to reasonable levels in our country the bastion of power that will be seriously affected is the bureaucracy. So it is natural for those people to object and to obstruct decentralisation from taking a definite shape.

Municipal sub-committees, DDC and other such similar bodies are still to be constituted in most states. To take up the work of decentralisation in right earnest bodies should be constituted and their roles clearly defined without any further delay.

Sub-movements of environmentalism, feminism, etc. should be taken note of and their beneficial influences on this process of decentralisation should be stressed so that the relation between such movements and decentralisation becomes one of symbiosis and not conflict. SFCs have not been constituted in most states; so financial decentralisation in these states has not begun. This process should be hastened and once these are constituted their recommendations should be made into law as soon as possible. As decentralisation naturally entails some erosion in the powers of the state and accretion in power of the newly formed DPCs naturally a tussle between the two will begin. Such conflicts have to be resolved.

As far as the planning process under a decentralised system is concerned specific guidelines are nowhere to be found resulting in chaos and a plethora of conflicting suggestions. All such suggestions have to be carefully studied to give a general structure to the planning exercise (for example block planning) also allowing for regional flexibilities in the true spirit of decentralisation.

The Official Secrets Act which gives the bureaucracy, specially the executive wing, right to function as they please without being responsible to the people has to be done away with if decentralisation has truly to be implemented. The Official Secrets Act breeds corruption, and transparency which is essential for the success of decentralisation is subverted. It is heartening to know that the present government is taking steps to tone down the power of this anachronistic act. Also the Pay Commission Report (Pandiyan Commission) has suggested such a measure. Another serious problem that impairs the smooth working of the decentralised planning mechanism is the lack of coordination between people's bodies and government officials. In the present set-up the funds for execution are given to lower bodies while the government official line-departments etc. have the infrastructure to execute plans. So naturally a problem arises whose roots are in a superiority complex of either party. This lack of coordination has to be somehow corrected and it is encouraging to know that steps in that direction are being taken.

Lack of political will has ever been a negative force pulling any well-thought out strategy for social development in the opposite direction. How political will can be changed to support decentralisation measures is still an open question that needs to be solved. Transparency in the functioning of lower bodies is of utmost importance for the success of decentralised planning and for fighting corruption. If transparency is not guaranteed in these bodies, corruption will strike its root and people's bodies will deteriorate to another slow moving bureaucracy with its own rules and self-defeating procedures. In West Bengal the formation of the non-elected lowermost bodies *Gram Sabha* and *Gram Samsad* is a step in the direction of ensuring transparency. These bodies can take part in people's audit, monitoring of work in progress, etc.

There are no clear guidelines for functioning of lower bodies in some cases (like use of funds) resulting in much confusion and duplication of work. These obstacles have to be removed and clear guidelines for duties have to be made.

In the fast globalising economy of India multi-national companies have a much important role to play. What will be their role as far as decentralised planning is concerned and will these be harmful or beneficial? A public debate on such issues has to be held and necessary steps taken forthwith.

Last but not the least, as decentralised planning is planning for the people and by the people, people from all walks of life should be motivated to get involved in the process. Scientists, sociologists, economists, bureaucrats and the common man should come forward to take up this holy task of nation building complementing each other with their individual expertise and knowledge in this great synergic movement towards sustainable human development of our motherland.

# BIBLIOGRAPHY


Babu, P.K. Krishna. *Regional Planning in India,* Chugh Publications, Allahabad, India.

Barbier, Edward B. *The Concept of Sustainable Development-Environmental Conservation.* Vol.14, No.2, 1987.

Bendavid-Val, Arrom, *Rural Area Development and Planning,* Food and Agriculture Organisation of the United Nations, Rome, 1990.

Chaturvedi, Anil. *District Administration—The Dynamics of Discord,* Sage Publications, New Delhi.

Daly, H.E. *The Economic Growth Debate:* What some ecomonist have earned but many have not, *Journal of Environmental Economics.* Vol.14, 1987.

Daly, H.E. *Sustainable Development from Concept and Theory toward Operational Principles,* Population and Development Review, Hoover Institution Conference.

Daly, H.E. and Cood, B. (Junior), For the Common Good: Restricting the Economy Toward Community the Environment and Development and a Sustainable Future, Beacon Press, Boston, 1989.

*Economic and Political Weekly,* Vol.xxx, no 35 and 40, dt. Sep 2 1995 and Oct. 10 1985.

*Encyclopedia of Social Work in India,* Ministry of Welfare, Government of India, vol. 1, 2.

Environment Management Training an ILO/UNEP Programme in support of Manager and Management Institution, Edited by Dr. R.G.A Boland, Sterling Publishers, New Delhi.

Friend J.K. and Jessop, W.N. *Local Govt. and Strategic Choice,* Pergamon Press.

*Human Development Report 1993, 94, 95, 96, 97,* UNDP, Oxford University Press, New Delhi.

Kumar Ashok (Editor). *Developing Women and Children in India,* Commonwealth Publishers, New Delhi.

Mallick Ross, *Development Policy of A Communist*, Cambridge University Press.

Mishra, R. P. (Editor) *Local Level Planning and Development,* Sterling Publishers Pvt. Limited, N. Delhi.

Nagaseshana, Pradhan, Thapliyal, Tripathi and Verma, *Block Plan in the District Frame*, National Institute of Rural Development, Rejendra Nagar, Hyderabad.

Pearce, David, Anil Markandya and Edward B. Barbier, *Blue Print for a Green Economy,* Earthscan Publication Ltd., 1989, London.

Pearce, David, Edward Barbier and Anil Markandya, *Sustainable Development Economics and Environment in the Third World*, Edward Elger Publishing/Earthscan Publications, 1990.

Pezey Jho (1989), *Economic Analysis of Sustainble Growth and Sustainable Development,* Environment Development Working, Paper no. 15, World Bank, Washington.

Prasad, V. Sivalikya. *Panchayat and Development,* Light and Life Publishers, New Delhi.

Rao, V. Bhaskar, Ramulu, C.H. Bala, *Development Strategies in India,* Khanna Publishers, New Delhi.

Rao, M. Vivekananda, *Planning Unit Areas for Interested Rural Development: An Exercise,* Ashish Publishing House, New Delhi.

Redclift, M. (1989), *Sustainable Development : Exploring the Contradictions*, Methuen, New York.

Ready, G. Narayan and Readdy, Suma Narayan, *Woman and Child Development (some contemporary issues),* Chugh Publications, Allahabad, India.

Ross, William F. (1989), *Defining Sustainable Development*, CHS Research Bulletin, University of British Colombia.

Singh, Katar, *Rural Development, Principles, Policies and Management,* Sage Publications, New Delhi.

Sinha, R.K., *Planning in India–A Critique,* South Asian Publishers, New Delhi.

*State Finance Commision—Summary of Recommendations and Action Taken Report* (Govt. of West Bengal).

# INDEX